LISTEN TO ME!

Beginning Listening Comprehension

Barbara H. Foley

Institute for Intensive English
Union County College, New Jersey

NEWBURY HOUSE PUBLISHERS
A division of HarperCollins*Publishers*

Cover and interior book design by Diana Esterly

Illustrations by Dan Reeves

NEWBURY HOUSE PUBLISHERS
A division of HarperCollins*Publishers*

Language Science
Language Teaching
Language Learning

First printing: February 1985
11 12 13 14 15

Printed in the U.S.A.

INTRODUCTION

Listen to Me! is intended for beginning and high beginning students of English as a second language. It is both a listening comprehension and a listening discrimination program. Its purpose is to develop effective listening skills for high interest narratives and conversations.

The emphasis throughout the units is on listening in context. As they follow each selection, students hear the sound and flow of English. They hear the organization of the language and the sequence and relationship of ideas. They hear new vocabulary in a meaningful setting. As students concentrate on the message, the sense of the language becomes clearer to them.

Listen to Me! seeks to improve four listening skills: 1) determining vocabulary meaning from visual cues and from context; 2) following a main idea with supporting details; 3) listening for a specific purpose; and 4) recognizing specific grammatical structures within a setting.

The book contains twenty units, each with a narrative and a conversation. Each unit describes a particular person, focusing on his or her job, dreams or problems. Each unit begins with a full-page illustration of the story, often consisting of several small pictures which show the sequence of events or flow of the story. Students may wish to look at this page for a few minutes before beginning the unit. Most of the units follow the format outlined below. The suggested procedure for completing each unit is as follows:

LISTENING COMPREHENSION

A. **Discussion**   The questions in this section introduce the topic to the class. They provide a schema for the topic and arouse the student's interest in the selection. At the outset, teachers should encourage students to offer information, personal stories, and opinions. The focus here is on developing a background for listening to the passage.

B. **Vocabulary**   The class should discuss the new words before hearing them on the tape. Then, the teacher may ask the students for other examples. The teacher should say the vocabulary words and ask the students to repeat each one. Where possible, the teacher should ask the students to point out the object or action in the illustrations.

C. **First Listening** Students listen to the taped story while following the illustrations. The tape, or parts of it, may be played as many times as the class requests. Students who do not understand the complete story will be aided by the illustrations. After listening, the students tell the class any information they remember about the story. The focus here is not on grammer but on the comprehension of the story. One student may only be able to give back one small piece of information. Another may be able to remember several facts. The teacher should prompt students to recall most of the information, especially those parts which are pictured. Students who may have had difficulty understanding the selection will learn from their classmates. Their comprehension will improve with each playing of the tape.

D. **Listen and Choose** (or Order) This exercise may ask the class to listen to the taped story again, this time with a specific task in mind. Students may be asked to record figures, put events in sequence, check the items a person bought, and so forth.

E. **Listen and Number** or **Listen for Numbers** This activity usually asks students to identify specific story pictures. While looking at the illustration page, the students hear statements from the story. They must decide which picture the statement is describing. Occasionally, they must answer questions with a correct number or amount from the story and pictures.

F. **True or False** In this exercise, students listen to statements about the story. They need to determine if the statement is true or false. Because the statements are heard and not read, the teacher may need to play some statements more than once.

G. **Word Groups** This is a word association activity. Students will need an introduction to this type of exercise. In order to explain it to the class, the teacher should write a general word on the blackboard, such as *school,* then ask students what they think of when they hear this word. Responses might include *teacher, book, study, classroom, test, homework, bus,* and so forth. Other general words which may be used as examples are *love, children* and *house.* Then as they listen to the story, students try to write words they can associate with those in Word Groups.

H. **Listen and STOP!** In this activity, students listen for sentences which are similar in meaning. The students read the exercise sentences to themselves. Then, the teacher replays the tape. When students hear a sentence that means almost the same as the sentence in the exercise, they tell the teacher to STOP! the tape. The teacher should then ask one student to repeat the taped sentence. The sentences are in the same order as they appear in the story.

I. **On Your Own** or **With a Group**   These activities give students an opportunity to relate the topic of the unit to their own lives. The instructions vary with the activity. Those labeled *With a Group* usually work best in small groups of three or four students.

LISTENING DISCRIMINATION

Throughout the unit so far, the concentration has been on content. Now the concentration is on structure through listening discrimination exercises. Each unit focuses on a particular verb tense. Although there is a variety of tenses within each selection, one tense predominates. Students are now asked to consider its usage in several sentences from the taped story. In all exercises, students should immediately check their own answers. For some of the exercises, the teacher replays the tape, asking the students which form they heard or which verb they wrote. There are several exercise types in this section:

J. (or **K.**) **Listen and Circle**   In this exercise, students listen for verb forms. After listening to a sentence, they circle the verb they hear. In a variation of this exercise, students hear two sentences. They must determine if they are the same or different.

K. (or **L.**) **Listen and Write**   Students listen to sentences from the story and are asked to write the complete verb. Teachers can stop the tape after each item if students need additional writing time. The teacher should replay the tape and have the students check their answers.

L. and **M. Fill In**/Completion or Choice exercises   Students must complete sentences from the story with the correct form of the verb, complete sentences with various grammatical elements (articles, pronouns, singular and plural nouns, and so forth) or choose the correct grammatical element that they hear on the tape (verb forms, singular and plural nouns, short answers, articles, and so forth).

N. **Prepositions**   Students fill in the correct prepositions in sentences which are taken from the story.

CONVERSATION

O. **Listen** Students listen to a conversation between two of the people in or related to the taped story. Then they answer general comprehension questions about the conversation.

P. **Synonyms** Students listen again to find synonyms in the conversation that match the words and expressions listed in the text.

Q. **Complete the Conversation** Entering the conversation, the student becomes one of the two people and writes his/her lines while listening again to the tape.

CONTENTS

III. Present Tense

IV. Past Tense

LISTEN TO ME!

I.
Present "to be"

LISTENING COMPREHENSION

A. Discuss these questions with your class.

Do you live in a house or in an apartment? Do you know your neighbors? Do you talk with them a lot? What countries are they from? What do they do?

B. Vocabulary Talk about the new vocabulary words. If possible, point out the items in the story pictures. Repeat each word after the teacher.

aunt and uncle	*single*
apartment building	*retired*
telephone operator	*a couple*
twins	*x-ray technician*

C. First Listening Look at the pictures and listen to the story as many times as you want. After you listen, tell the class any information you remember about the story.

D. Listen and Choose Listen to the story again. Match each person with his or her occupation.

Ali	telephone operator
Mr. Ramirez	student
Mrs. Ramirez	x-ray technician
Mr. Pali	mailman
Cao	retired teacher
Ha	student

E.   Listen and Number   Look at the pictures and answer these questions with the correct number.

1. _____   5. _____

2. _____   6. _____

3. _____   7. _____

4. _____   8. _____

F.   True or False   Listen to these statements. Write T if the statement is true, F if the statement is false.

1. _____   6. _____

2. _____   7. _____

3. _____   8. _____

4. _____   9. _____

5. _____   10. _____

G.   Word Groups   Listen to the story again. As you listen, write a few words which you can put in each group.

Family   *School*

aunt   *university*

_____   _____

_____   _____

_____   _____

H.   Listen and STOP!   Read these sentences. Then listen to the tape again. When you hear a sentence that means almost the same as each sentence below, tell your teacher to stop the tape.

 1. I go to school.
 2. Four families live in this building.
 3. A husband and wife and their two children live under us.
 4. They have two sons.
 5. He lives by himself.
 6. Mr. Pali is almost 70.
 7. Mr. Pali isn't working now.
 8. There is a husband and wife from Vietnam.
 9. Cao and I go to school together.
10. The people here are nice.

I.   On Your Own   Write the name of one of your neighbors.

_____

Now, write a few sentences about this neighbor.

_____

_____

_____

_____

LISTENING DISCRIMINATION

J.   Listen and Circle   Listen to these sentences from the story. Circle the verb you hear.

1. is	am	are	6. is	am	are
2. is	am	are	7. is	am	are
3. is	am	are	8. is	am	are
4. is	am	are	9. is	am	are
5. is	am	are	10. is	am	are

K. **Listen and Write** Listen to these sentences from the story. Write the verb you hear.

1. _____   6. _____

2. _____   7. _____

3. _____   8. _____

4. _____   9. _____

5. _____   10. _____

L. **There and They** Listen to these sentences from the story. How does each sentence begin? Circle the first two words of each sentence.

1. There's   There are   They are

2. There's   There are   They are

3. There's   There are   They are

4. There's   There are   They are

5. There's   There are   They are

6. There's   There are   They are

7. There's   There are   They are

8. There's   There are   They are

M. Complete Complete these sentences with "There is," "There are," or "They are."

1. _____ a single man next to us.

2. _____ good neighbors.

3. _____ four families in this building.

4. _____ a family of four living under us.

5. _____ twins.

6. _____ ten years old.

7. _____ a couple from Vietnam in the fourth apartment.

N. Prepositions Complete these sentences with the correct preposition.

1. I'm _____ Egypt.

2. I'm a student _____ Oakdale University.

3. There's a family of four living _____ us.

4. Manuel and Mario are _____ the fourth grade.

5. _____ _____ us, there is a single man.

6. I think he's _____ 68 years old.

7. _____ the fourth apartment, there's a young couple _____

 Vietnam.

8. We're _____ the same English class.

9. We walk _____ school together.

10. All the people _____ my apartment building are friendly.

CONVERSATION

O. Listen to the conversation a few times. Then, answer these questions.

Who is talking?
Where are they?
Are they really late? Explain.
Where is the teacher?
When is the next class?
What are Ali and Cao going to do?

P. **Synonyms** Listen to the conversation again. Write a word that means almost the same as the words below.

not early _____

Did you forget? _____

Of course! _____

Q. **Complete the Conversation**   The teacher may play the conversation several times.

Cao: _____

Ali: It's me, Ali. Let's go!

Cao: _____

Ali: Come on. We're late.

Cao: _____

_____

Ali: Oh! That's right! I forgot.

Cao: _____

_____

Ali: O.K. Sounds good.

BACK IN SCHOOL

2

LISTENING COMPREHENSION

A. Discuss these questions with your class.

What is the name of your school? What class are you in? What other classes are there at your school?

How many students are in your class? What countries are they from?

B. **Vocabulary** Talk about the new vocabulary words. If possible, point out the items in the story pictures. Repeat each word after the teacher.

nervous	*patient*
each other	*break*
neighbor	*cafeteria*
fast	*homework*

C. **First Listening** Look at the pictures and listen to the story as many times as you want. After you listen, tell the class any information you remember about the story.

D. **Listen and Choose** People study English for many reasons. Check the reasons that this student is going to school.

_____ 1. to understand her children

_____ 2. to get a job.

_____ 3. to talk to her children's teachers

_____ 4. to talk to her husband

_____ 5. to go to college.

_____ 6. to learn to type

_____ 7. to talk to her children's friends

11

E. **Listen for Numbers**   There are many numbers in this story. Answer each question with the correct number.

1. _____	7. _____
2. _____	8. _____
3. _____	9. _____
4. _____	10. _____
5. _____	11. _____
6. _____	12. _____

F. **True or False**   Listen to these statements. Write T if the statement is true, F if the statement is false.

1. _____	6. _____
2. _____	7. _____
3. _____	8. _____
4. _____	9. _____
5. _____	10. _____

G. **Word Groups**   Listen to the story again. As you listen, write a few words which you can put in each group.

School

Classes
_____

_____

_____

_____

People

adult
_____

_____

_____

_____

H. **Listen and STOP!** Read these sentences. Then listen to the tape again. When you hear a sentence that means almost the same as each sentence below, tell the teacher to stop the tape.

1. There are different classes.
2. My room number is 201.
3. I don't understand English.
4. English is not easy for me.
5. It's important for me to learn English.
6. All my children are in school.
7. Many students are from Mexico.
8. There are four students from other countries.
9. Our teacher is good.
10. I go to school all morning.

I. **With a Group**

A. Why do you want to learn English? Tell the other students your reasons.

B. Answer these questions about your class.

1. What's today's date? _____

2. What is the room number? _____

3. How many students are in your class? _____

4. What countries are the students from? How many are from

   each country?

   _____   _____

   _____   _____

   _____   _____

   _____   _____

   _____   _____

5. How many days a week do you come to school?

   _____

6. How long is the class? _____

7. What time does school begin? _____

8. What time does school end? _____

9. What time is your break? _____

10. What is your teacher's name? _____

LISTENING DISCRIMINATION

J. Listen and Circle Listen to these sentences from the story. Circle the verb you hear.

1. a. am   b. is   c. are

2. a. am   b. is   c. are

3. a. am   b. is   c. are

4. a. am   b. is   c. are

5. a. am   b. is   c. are

6. a. am   b. is   c. are

7. a. am   b. is   c. are

8. a. am   b. is   c. are

9. a. am   b. is   c. are

10. a. am   b. is   c. are

K. Listen and Write Listen to these sentences from the story. Write the verb you hear.

1. _____   6. _____

2. _____   7. _____

3. _____   8. _____

4. _____   9. _____

5. _____   10. _____

L. **Fill In**   Complete these sentences from the story with "is," "am," or "are."

   1. This _____ the Dallas Adult School.

   2. My class _____ in Room 201.

   3. I _____ in Beginning English.

   4. Maybe I _____ too old to learn.

   5. I _____ 40 years old.

   6. Six students _____ like me, they _____ from Mexico.

   7. Sonia, my sister, _____ in my class.

   8. The teacher _____ patient with all of us.

   9. Our class _____ three hours every day.

   10. I _____ happy that I _____ back in school.

M. **Fill In**   Complete these sentences with the correct word from the list below.

        they   their   there

   1. _____ are classes for math, reading, and typing.

   2. And _____ are classes for English.

   3. _____ all speak English.

   4. Sometimes, _____ speak English to each other, and I don't

      understand them.

   5. I want to talk to _____ friends and I want to talk to

      _____ teachers.

   6. _____ are ten students in our class.

   7. Six are like me, _____ 're from Mexico.

   8. _____ are three students from Vietnam.

   9. _____ 's a break at 10:30.

N. **Prepositions** Complete these sentences with the correct preposition.

1. It's the second week _____ school.

2. My class is _____ Room 201.

3. This is my fourth year _____ the United States.

4. I'm a little nervous _____ school.

5. English is difficult _____ me.

6. This year my four children are _____ school.

7. My sister is _____ my class.

8. There are three students _____ Vietnam and one _____ India.

9. Our teacher is patient _____ all _____ us.

10. Our class is _____ 9:00 _____ 12:00.

CONVERSATION

O. Listen to the conversation a few times. Then, answer these questions.

> Who is talking?
> Who are they talking about?
> Why is he absent?
> What kind of student is he?
> What is Mrs. Lang doing?

P. **Synonyms** Listen to the conversation again. Write a word that means almost the same as the words below.

not well _____

problem _____

telephoned _____

homework _____

feeling well _____

Q. **Complete the Conversation** The teacher may play the conversation several times.

Student: _____

Carmen: Mr. Torres is sick today.

Student: _____

Carmen: He called me this morning. He has a bad cold.

Student: _____

Carmen: Yes. He's upset because he's not in school. But, Ms. Lang is

giving me his papers.

Student: _____

1. MEMORIAL HOSPITAL

2. THEATER RESTAURANT MUSEUM

3. 17,000.00

4. APARTMENT FOR RENT $600.00 per month

5. GENERAL HOSPITAL

6.

7. PAY TO THE ORDER 14,000.00

8. FOR RENT 300.00 PER MONTH

CITY OR COUNTRY?

LISTENING COMPREHENSION

A. Discuss these questions with your class.

Is there a hospital in your area? How large is it? What kind of hospital is it?

B. **Vocabulary** Talk about the new vocabulary words. If possible, point out the items in the story pictures. Repeat each word after the teacher.

nursing school | patients
graduate | salary
offers | general
cancer | choose

C. **First Listening** Look at the pictures and listen to the story as many times as you want. After you listen, tell the class any information you remember about the story.

D. **Listen and Choose** Read each statement. Is it about the city hospital or the country hospital? Write "city" or "country" after each sentence.

1. It's a 600-bed hospital. _____

2. It's near the mountains. _____

3. It takes care of all kinds of patients. _____

4. The salary is high. _____

5. It's a general hospital. _____

6. The salary is average. _____

7. It's a cancer hospital. _____

8. It's a 50-bed hospital. _____

E. Listen and Number   Listen to these sentences from the story. Write in the number of the correct picture.

1. _____   6. _____

2. _____   7. _____

3. _____   8. _____

4. _____   9. _____

5. _____   10. _____

F. True or False   Listen to these statements. Write T if the statement is true, F if the statement is false.

1. _____   6. _____

2. _____   7. _____

3. _____   8. _____

4. _____   9. _____

5. _____   10. _____

G. Word Groups   Listen to the story again. As you listen, write a few words which you can put in each group.

City   *Country*

museums   *lakes*

_____   _____

_____   _____

_____   _____

H. **Listen and STOP!**   Read these sentences. Then listen to the tape again. When you hear a sentence that means almost the same as each sentence below, tell the teacher to stop the tape.

1. Gloria is studying to be a nurse.
2. Two hospitals are interested in Gloria.
3. The city hospital is big.
4. The hospital is near entertainment.
5. It's expensive to rent an apartment.
6. It takes care of everyone who is sick.
7. The salary isn't high, but it isn't low.
8. Gloria can't decide what to do.

I. **On Your Own**   Complete this chart, which compares the city hospital and the country hospital.

City	Country
large	_____
600-bed	_____
_____	general
near museums, theaters, and restaurants	_____
	_____
	_____
_____	$14,000
_____	apartment rents are low

LISTENING DISCRIMINATION

J.   Listen and Circle   Listen to these sentences from the story. Circle
the verb you hear.

1. is	are	6. is	are
2. is	are	7. is	are
3. is	are	8. is	are
4. is	are	9. is	are
5. is	are	10. is	are

K.   Listen and Write   Listen to these sentences from the story. Write
the verb you hear, "is" or "are."

1. _____   6. _____

2. _____   7. _____

3. _____   8. _____

4. _____   9. _____

5. _____   10. _____

L.   Singular or Plural   Listen to these sentences. Do you hear a
singular or plural noun? Circle the word you hear.

1. a. offer, b. offers

2. a. hospital, b. hospitals

3. a. patient, b. patients

4. a. city, b. cities, c. museum, d. museums

5. a. rent, b. rents

6. a. hospital, b. hospitals

7. a. kind, b. kinds

8. a. lake, b. lakes

9. a. salary, b. salaries

10. a. hospital, b. hospitals

M. Fill In Read these sentences. Write in the correct noun in the singular or the plural.

1. It's a big hospital, near _____ (restaurant, restaurants).

2. It's a 600-bed _____ (hospital, hospitals).

3. It's in a big _____ (city, cities).

4. It takes care of all kinds of _____ (patient, patients).

5. It's in a beautiful _____ (area, areas), near _____

   (mountain, mountains).

6. Apartment _____ (rent, rents) are high.

N. Prepositions Complete these sentences with the correct preposition.

1. Gloria is a student _____ nursing school.

2. She has two job offers. One is _____ a city hospital, the other is

   _____ a country hospital.

3. It gives excellent care _____ its patients.

4. It's _____ a big city, _____ museums and restaurants.

5. It takes care _____ all kinds _____ patients.

6. It's _____ a beautiful area.

CONVERSATION

O.   Listen to the conversation a few times. Then, answer these questions.

> Who's talking?
> Where are they?
> Where does Gloria's mother want her to work?
> What are her reasons?
> What is Gloria going to do?

P.   **Synonyms**   Listen to the conversation again. Write a word that means almost the same as the words below.

mother   _____

close   _____

a long way   _____

not leaving   _____

Q. **Complete the Conversation** The teacher may play the conversation several times.

Gloria: _____

Mother: Well, you know, we'd like you near us.

Gloria: _____

Mother: And the country is so far from here.

Gloria: _____

Mother: And you'd need a car in the country.

Gloria: _____

Mother: And all your friends are here.

Gloria: _____

Mother: And what about David?

Gloria: _____

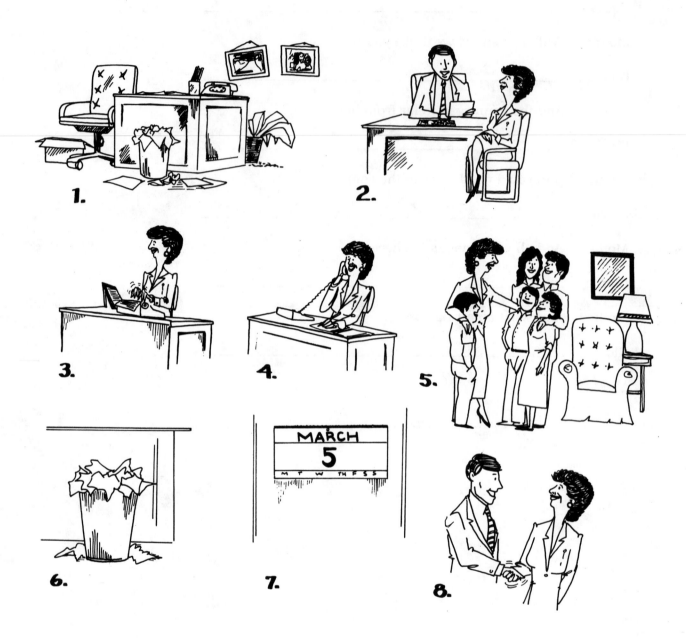

1.

2.

3.

4.

5.

6.

7.

8.

THE JOB INTERVIEW

LISTENING COMPREHENSION

A. Discuss these questions with your class.

What is a job interview? What are some questions an interviewer asks at a job interview? Did you ever have a job interview? If so, describe it to the class.

B. **Vocabulary** Talk about the new vocabulary words. If possible, point out the items in the story pictures. Repeat each word after the teacher.

boss   experience
mess   typing course
in order   organized
interview   take care of

C. **First Listening** Look at the pictures and listen to the story as many times as you want. After you listen, tell the class any information you remember about the story.

D. **Listen and Choose** Mrs. Santana says that she is the right person for this job. What are her abilities? Check her abilities as you listen to the story again.

_____ 1. She's friendly on the telephone.

_____ 2. She's young.

_____ 3. She's a good typist.

_____ 4. She's a good driver.

_____ 5. She's a secretary with many years of experience.

_____ 6. She's a hard worker.

_____ 7. She's organized.

E. **Listen and Number** Listen to these sentences from the story. Write in the number of the correct picture.

1. _____   6. _____

2. _____   7. _____

3. _____   8. _____

4. _____   9. _____

5. _____   10. _____

F. **True or False** Listen to these statements. Write T if the statement is true, F if the statement is false.

1. _____   6. _____

2. _____   7. _____

3. _____   8. _____

4. _____   9. _____

5. _____   10. _____

G. **Word Groups** Listen to the story again. As you listen, write a few words which you can put in each group.

Office   *People*

papers _____   *secretary* _____

_____   _____

_____   _____

_____   _____

_____   _____

H. **Listen and STOP!** Read these sentences. Then listen to the tape again. When you hear a sentence that means almost the same as each sentence below, tell the teacher to stop the tape.

1. Mr. Johnson is the president of this company.
2. Things are all over his desk and his office.
3. He doesn't have a secretary.
4. She isn't a young woman.
5. I know how to type very well.
6. I have five children.
7. My house is neat.
8. There are papers up to the top of your basket.
9. Your calendar is five days behind.
10. What day can you begin?

I. **On Your Own** What are your job abilities? What can you do? Complete this job information about yourself. Then, show it to your teacher.

1. I'm _____ .

2. I'm _____ .

3. I'm _____ .

4. I can _____ .

5. I can _____ .

6. I can _____ .

With a Group Write seven questions that an interviewer asks on a job interview. Then, ask each of the students in the group all the questions.

1. _____ ?

2. _____ ?

3. _____ ?

4. _____ ?

5. _____ ?

6. _____ ?

7. _____ ?

LISTENING DISCRIMINATION

J. Listen and Circle Listen to these sentences from the story. Circle the verb you hear.

1. a. am   b. is   c. are

2. a. am   b. is   c. are

3. a. am   b. is   c. are

4. a. am   b. is   c. are

5. a. am   b. is   c. are

6. a. am   b. is   c. are

7. a. am   b. is   c. are

8. a. am   b. is   c. are

9. a. am   b. is   c. are

10. a. am   b. is   c. are

K. Listen and Write Listen to these sentences from the story. Write the verb you hear.

1. _____   6. _____

2. _____   7. _____

3. _____   8. _____

4. _____   9. _____

5. _____   10. _____

L.   Fill In   Complete these sentences from the story with "am," "is," or "are."

1. Mr. Johnson _____ the boss of Acme Trucking.

2. There _____ papers and books everywhere.

3. Nothing _____ in order.

4. Mrs. Santana _____ an older woman.

5. I _____ a good typist.

6. I _____ the right person for this job.

7. Your basket _____ full.

8. Papers _____ everywhere.

9. Today _____ the tenth.

10. I _____ a hard worker.

M.   Singular or Plural   Listen to these sentences. Do you hear a singular or plural noun? Circle the word you hear.

1. a. book, b. books, c. box, d. boxes

2. a. secretary, b. secretaries

3. a. woman, b. women

4. a. experience, b. experiences

5. a. typist, b. typists

6. a. course, b. courses

7. a. word, b. words

8. a. child, b. children

9. a. paper, b. papers

10. a. basket, b. baskets

N. Prepositions Complete these sentences with the correct preposition.

1. Mr. Johnson is the boss _____ Acme Trucking.

2. She's _____ his office _____ an interview.

3. I'm the right person _____ this job.

4. I'm friendly _____ the telephone.

5. I'm the mother _____ five children.

6. The date _____ your calendar is the fifth.

7. I can take care of everything _____ your office.

CONVERSATION

O.   Listen to the conversation a few times. Then, answer these questions.

> Who's talking?
> Where are they?
> When does Mrs. Santana start her new job?
> How many trucks does the company have?
> What is Mrs. Santana's job?
> What are they going to do this evening?

P.   **Synonyms**   Listen to the conversation again. Write a word that means almost the same as the words below.

begin	_____
little	_____
vans	_____
put in order	_____
eat out	_____

Q.   **Complete the Conversation**   The teacher may play the conversation several times.

Mrs. Santana: I got it! I got the job!

Mr. Santana: _____

Mrs. Santana: Yes. I start on Monday.

Mr. Santana: _____

Mrs. Santana: Well, it's a small company. It's a moving company.

They have ten trucks.

Mr. Santana: _____

Mrs. Santana: I answer the telephone, type orders, and organize

the office.

Mr. Santana: _____

II.
Present Continuous Tense

1.

2.

3.

4.

5.

6.

7.

8.

9.

10.

BLOWING A FUSE

LISTENING COMPREHENSION

A. Discuss these questions with your class.

What's a fuse? What happens when you blow a fuse? Where is the fuse box in your house or apartment?

B. **Vocabulary** Talk about the new vocabulary words. If possible, point out the items in the story pictures. Repeat each word after the teacher.

coffee maker	blow dryer
piece of bread	blew a fuse
toaster	basement
blow drying	flashlight

C. **First Listening** Look at the pictures and listen to the story as many times as you want. After you listen, tell the class any information you remember about the story.

D. **Listen and Choose** Where is each person or object in this story? Match each with the correct room.

Ann	in the basement
the iron	in the bathroom
Larry	in the kitchen
the toaster	in the bathroom
Mrs. Benton	in the kitchen
the blow dryer	in the living room
the fuse box	in the living room

E. Listen and Number   Listen to these sentences from the story. Which picture is each one describing? Write in the number of the correct picture.

1. _____   6. _____

2. _____   7. _____

3. _____   8. _____

4. _____   9. _____

5. _____   10. _____

F. True or False   Listen to these statements. Write T if the statement is true, F if the statement is false.

1. _____   6. _____

2. _____   7. _____

3. _____   8. _____

4. _____   9. _____

5. _____   10. _____

G. Word Groups   Listen to the story again. As you listen, write a few words which you can put in each group.

Places   *Electric*

school   coffee maker

_____   _____

_____   _____

_____   _____

H. Listen and STOP! Read these sentences. Then listen to the tape again. When you hear a sentence that means almost the same as each sentence below, tell the teacher to stop the tape.

1. No one is sleeping.
2. The children are preparing for school.
3. Mr. Benton is making coffee.
4. His daughter is in the same room.
5. Larry is fixing his hair.
6. The radio is off.
7. There's no electricity.
8. Mr. Benton is putting in a new fuse.

I. On Your Own

1. List five appliances you have in your house. Tell which room each one is in.

toaster   *kitchen*

television   *living room*

_____   _____

_____   _____

_____   _____

_____   _____

2. Imagine that it's 7:00 in the morning at your house. What are you doing? What is each person in your family doing?

_____

_____

_____

_____

_____

LISTENING DISCRIMINATION

J.   **Listen and Circle**   Listen to these sentences from the story. Circle the verb you hear.

    1. a. is   b. are

    2. a. is getting   b. are getting

    3. a. is getting   b. are getting

    4. a. is fixing   b. are fixing

    5. a. is putting   b. are putting

    6. a. is listening   b. are listening

    7. a. is   b. are

    8. a. is blow drying   b. are blow drying

    9. a. is   b. are

   10. a. is   b. are

K.   **Listen and Write**   Listen to these sentences from the story. Write the verb you hear.

1. _____   6. _____

2. _____   7. _____

3. _____   8. _____

4. _____   9. _____

5. _____   10. _____

L.   Fill In   Complete these sentences from the story with a verb in the present continuous tense.

1. Mr. and Mrs. Benton _____ _____ ready for work.

2. Mr. Benton _____ _____ coffee in the coffee maker.

3. Ann _____ _____ a piece of bread into the toaster.

4. They _____ both _____ to the radio.

5. Mrs. Benton _____ _____ her blouse.

6. Larry _____ _____ his hair.

7. The coffee maker _____ n't _____ .

8. Mrs. Benton _____ _____ at the iron.

9. Mr. Benton _____ _____ down to the basement.

10. He _____ _____ the fuse.

M.   Fill In   Complete these sentences with the correct word from the list below.

> he   his
> she   her
> they

1. Mr. Benton is in the kitchen. _____ 's fixing coffee.

2. Ann is there, too. _____ 's putting a piece of bread in the

   toaster.

3. _____ 're both listening to the radio.

4. Mrs. Benton is ironing _____ blouse.

5. Larry is blow drying _____ hair.

6. Mr. Benton is going down the basement with _____ flash-

   light.

7. _____ 's changing the fuse.

N.   Prepositions   Complete these sentences with the correct preposition.

1. Everyone is awake _____ the Benton's.

2. Mr. Benton is _____ the kitchen.

3. Larry and Ann are getting ready _____ school.

4. She's putting a piece of bread _____ the toaster.

5. Larry is _____ the bathroom.

6. There is no music _____ the radio.

7. Mr. Benton is going_____ to the basement _____ his flashlight.

CONVERSATION

O.   Listen to the conversation a few times. Then, answer these questions.

Who is calling out to Mr. Benton? What is each person saying?
Does Mr. Benton know immediately that they blew a fuse?
Where is the flashlight?
What is Mr. Benton doing?
Why did they blow a fuse?

P.   Synonyms   Listen to the conversation again. Write a word that means almost the same as the words below.

what's wrong   _____

I'm not sure   _____

becoming   _____

take it easy   _____

put in a new one   _____

Q.   Complete the Conversation   The teacher may play the conversation several times.

Mr. Benton: Hm, what's the matter with the radio?

Ann: _____

Larry: _____

Mrs. Benton: _____

Mr. Benton: Relax, everyone. We blew a fuse. Where's the flashlight?

Ann: _____

Mr. Benton: Thanks. I'll go down and change the fuse. We can't use so many appliances at the same time.

THE SUPERMARKET

LISTENING COMPREHENSION

A. Discuss these questions with your class.

Which supermarket do you shop at? How often do you go to the supermarket? Do you make a list before you go?

B. **Vocabulary** Talk about the new vocabulary words. If possible, point out the items in the story pictures. Repeat each word after the teacher.

manager	*produce*
service counter	*bunch*
cart	*knocked over*
aisles	*mopping*

C. **First Listening** Look at the pictures and listen to the story as many times as you want. After you listen, tell the class any information you remember about the story.

D. **Listen and Choose** In the story, there are the names of many foods. Put a check before each food that is in Mrs. Gomez's cart.

_____ chicken	_____ doughnuts
_____ ice cream	_____ bananas
_____ cookies	_____ grapes
_____ potato chips	_____ soda

E. **Listen and Number** Listen to these sentences from the story. Write the number of the picture in the correct space.

1. _____   6. _____

2. _____   7. _____

3. _____   8. _____

4. _____   9. _____

5. _____   10. _____

F. **True or False** Listen to these statements. Write T if the statement is true, F if the statement is false.

1. _____   6. _____

2. _____   7. _____

3. _____   8. _____

4. _____   9. _____

5. _____   10. _____

G. **Word Groups** Listen to the story again. As you listen, write a few words which you can put in each group.

Supermarket   *Food*

*Cart*_____   *meat*_____

_____   _____

_____   _____

_____   _____

_____   _____

H. **Listen and STOP!**   Read these sentences. Then listen to the tape again. When you hear a sentence that means almost the same as each sentence below, tell the teacher to stop the tape.

1. Mrs. Gomez and her family are coming into the supermarket.
2. The same thing happens every Friday night.
3. Mrs. Gomez is looking at the chicken.
4. Marco is adding his favorite foods.
5. He's saying, "Don't eat the bananas."
6. An angry clerk is holding Juan's arm.
7. Someone is cleaning up the floor.
8. She's leaving the store with her children.
9. "We'll be back next Friday."

I. **With a Group**

A. This story spoke about two departments in the supermarket, the meat department and the produce department. Write the names of four other departments. List three foods that are in that department.

Department   *Food*

1. _____: a. _____   b. _____   c. _____

2. _____: a. _____   b. _____   c. _____

3. _____: a. _____   b. _____   c. _____

4. _____: a. _____   b. _____   c. _____

B. Write the names of ten items that you buy in the store every week. Compare your lists. Check those items that everyone has on his or her list.

1. _____   6. _____

2. _____   7. _____

3. _____   8. _____

4. _____   9. _____

5. _____   10. _____

LISTENING DISCRIMINATION

J. Listen and Circle   You will hear two sentences. Decide if they are the same or different. Circle S or D. Listen for "is."

1. S   D   6. S   D

2. S   D   7. S   D

3. S   D   8. S   D

4. S   D   9. S   D

5. S   D   10. S   D

K. Listen and Write   Listen to these sentences from the story. Write the verb you hear. Two of the verbs are negative.

1. _____   6. _____

2. _____   7. _____

3. _____   8. _____

4. _____   9. _____

5. _____   10. _____

L. Fill In   Complete these sentences from the story with a verb in the present continuous tense.

1. The supermarket manager _____ _____ them from

the service counter.

2. Aida, the youngest, _____ _____ in the cart.

3. Aida _____ _____ louder and louder.

4. Marco _____ _____ food in the cart when his mother

isn't looking.

5. The produce manager _____ _____ to Carmen.

6. He _____ _____ a bunch of grapes from her.

7. One of the employees _____ _____ toward the

manager.

8. She _____ _____ a child after her.

9. Mrs. Gomez _____ _____ out of the store.

10. Her children _____ _____ quietly behind her.

M. **Singular or Plural** Listen to these sentences. Is the noun
singular or plural? Circle the correct noun.

1. a. child, b. children

2. a. night, b. nights

3. a. aisle, b. aisles

4. a. chicken, b. chickens

5. a. food, b. foods

6. a. cookie, b. cookies

7. a. banana, b. bananas

8. a. bunch, b. bunches, c. grape, d. grapes

9. a. employee, b. employees

10. a. bottle, b. bottles, c. soda, d. sodas

N. **Prepositions** Complete these sentences with the correct preposition.

1. Here comes Mrs. Gomez _____ her four children.

2. The supermarket manager is watching them _____ the service

counter.

3. Aida, the youngest, is sitting _____ the cart.

4. Mrs. Gomez is _____ the meat counter.

5. Marco is putting food _____ the cart.

6. He's taking a bunch of grapes _____ Carmen.

7. One _____ the employees is walking _____ the manager.

8. She's pulling a child _____ her.

9. Mrs. Gomez is walking _____ _____ the store.

10. Her children are following quietly _____ her.

CONVERSATION

O. Listen to the conversation a few times. Then, answer these questions.

Who is talking?
What part of the supermarket are the speakers in?
What is the employee watching?
Is the manager watching the TV monitor, also?
What are the children doing?
What is the manager's opinion of Mrs. Gomez?

P. **Synonyms** Listen to the conversation again. Write a word that means almost the same as the words below.

     look at   _____

     what's going on   _____

     crying   _____

     bananas, apples, peaches   _____

     spilled   _____

Q. **Complete the conversation.** The teacher may play the conversation several times.

Manager: _____

Employee: Mrs. Gomez?

Manager: _____

Employee: Okay.

Manager: _____

Employee: You can hear that.

Manager: _____

Employee: You're right. He is.

Manager: _____

_____

Employee: Right again.

Manager: _____

Employee: Yeah. And he just knocked over some soda. How did

you know all that?

Manager: _____

1.

2.

3.

4.

5.

6.

THE DISCO

LISTENING COMPREHENSION

A. Discuss these questions with your class.

> Do you ever go to discos? Is there one in your city or town? What kind of music do they play? What kind of dancing is there? What do people wear?

B. Vocabulary Talk about the new vocabulary words. If possible, point out the items in the story pictures. Repeat each word after the teacher.

dance floor	*partner*
band	*staring*
loud	*toward*
someone else	

C. First Listening Look at the pictures and listen to the story as many times as you want. After you listen, tell the class any information you remember about the story.

D. Listen and Choose Olga is at the disco. Check what she is doing there.

_____ 1. drinking

_____ 2. dancing with her boyfriend

_____ 3. standing with her friend

_____ 4. looking for someone

_____ 5. eating

_____ 6. talking with her friends

E.   Listen and Number   Listen to these sentences from the story. Write the number of the picture in the correct space.

1. _____   6. _____

2. _____   7. _____

3. _____   8. _____

4. _____   9. _____

5. _____

F.   True or False   Listen to these statements. Write T if the statement is true, F if the statement is false.

1. _____   6. _____

2. _____   7. _____

3. _____   8. _____

4. _____   9. _____

5. _____   10. _____

G.   Word Groups   Listen to the story again. As you listen, write a few words which you can put in each group.

Disco   *Look*

_____*dance*_____   _____*watching*_____

_____   _____

_____   _____

_____   _____

H. **Listen and STOP!** Read these sentences. Then listen to the tape again. When you hear a sentence that means almost the same as each sentence below, tell the teacher to stop the tape.

1. I want to have fun.
2. A lot of people are at the bar.
3. Olga has a lot of friends at the disco.
4. The music is loud.
5. He's with another woman.
6. Olga is leaving.
7. The girl is leaving him.
8. He wants to dance with her.
9. They are both smiling.

I. **On Your Own** Olga is at the disco. Imagine that you are at a disco, too. Look around. What is happening?

Examples

A heavy man is smoking a cigarette.

Several people are sitting at a table, talking.

_____

_____

_____

_____

LISTENING DISCRIMINATION

J.   **Listen and Circle**   Listen to these sentences from the story. Circle the verb you hear.

1. a. standing   b. is standing   c. are standing

2. a. is   b. are

3. a. watching   b. isn't watching   c. aren't watching

4. a. looking   b. is looking   c. are looking

5. a. dancing   b. is dancing   c. are dancing

6. a. playing   b. is playing   c. are playing

7. a. going   b. is going   c. are going

8. a. stopping   b. is stopping   c. are stopping

9. a. walking   b. is walking   c. are walking

10. a. smiling   b. is smiling   c. are smiling

K.   **Listen and Write**   Listen to these sentences from the story. Write the verb you hear.

1. _____   6. _____

2. _____   7. _____

3. _____   8. _____

4. _____   9. _____

5. _____   10. _____

L. Fill In   Complete these sentences from the story with a verb in the present continuous tense.

1. Olga _____ _____ at the bar with her friend.

2. Olga _____ _____ at the dance floor.

3. The band _____ _____ a loud song.

4. Almost everyone _____ _____ .

5. The music _____ _____ .

6. His partner _____ _____ away!

7. He _____ _____ at Olga.

8. He _____ _____ toward her.

9. He _____ _____ her to dance.

10. Olga _____ _____ , and so _____ he.

M. Fill In   Complete these sentences with the correct word from the list below.

    he   his   him
    she   her   them

1. I'm going to dance with _____ again.

2. Olga is standing at the bar with _____ friend.

3. Many people are at the bar. Olga isn't watching _____ .

4. She's looking for someone special. Where is _____ ?

5. Then, she sees _____ dancing.

6. Who is _____ ?

7. Is she _____ girlfriend?

8. _____ partner is walking away.

9. He's walking toward _____ .

10. He's asking _____ to dance.

N.   **Prepositions**   Complete these sentences with the correct preposition.

1. I'm going to dance _____ him.

2. Olga is standing _____ the bar _____ her friend.

3. Many people are _____ the bar.

4. She knows lots _____ the people, but she's looking _____ someone special.

5. He's dancing _____ someone else.

6. He's staring _____ Olga.

7. He's walking _____ her.

8. As they walk _____ the dance floor, Olga is smiling.

CONVERSATION

O. Listen to the conversation a few times. Then, answer these questions.

Who's talking?
Where are they standing?
What color shirt is he wearing?
What is the other girl doing?
Where is he walking?
What is Olga going to do tonight?

P. **Synonyms** Listen to the conversation again. Write a word that means almost the same as the words below.

It doesn't matter. _____

leaving _____

Don't go. _____

over _____

wonderful _____

Q. **Complete the Conversation** The teacher may play the conversation several times.

Sonia: Do you see him? Is he here?

Olga: _____

Sonia: Look! Over there. Is that him in the blue shirt?

Olga: _____

Sonia: Who is she?

Olga: _____

Sonia: Wait. The song's ending. She's walking away.

Olga: _____

Sonia: Here he comes. Have a good time, Olga.

ON STRIKE 8

LISTENING COMPREHENSION

A. Discuss these questions with your class.

What is a strike? Why do workers go on strike? Do you belong to a union? Were you ever on strike? What were the reasons for the strike?

B. **Vocabulary** Talk about the new vocabulary words. If possible, point out the items in the story pictures. Repeat each word after the teacher.

hand out	*shouting*
signs	*demands*
sweating	*increase*
leader	*agreement*

C. **First Listening** Look at the pictures and listen to the story as many times as you want. After you listen, tell the class any information you remember about the story.

D. **Listen and Choose** The workers at this company are on strike. Listen to the story again. Check the reasons that they are on strike.

_____ They want an increase in pay.

_____ The factory is not safe.

_____ They want better health benefits.

_____ They want more sick days.

_____ They want to work fewer hours.

E. **Listen and Number** Look at the pictures and listen to the tape. Answer these questions with the correct number. Your answer can be "none."

1. _____   6. _____

2. _____   7. _____

3. _____   8. _____

4. _____   9. _____

5. _____   10. _____

F. **True or False** Listen to these statements. Write T if the statement is true, F if the statement is false.

1. _____   6. _____

2. _____   7. _____

3. _____   8. _____

4. _____   9. _____

5. _____   10. _____

G. **Word Groups** Listen to the story again. As you listen, write a few words which you can put in each group.

Cold   *Hot*

snowing   *sweating*

_____   _____

_____   _____

_____   _____

_____   _____

H. **Listen and STOP!**   Read these sentences. Then listen to the tape again. When you hear a sentence that means almost the same as each sentence below, tell the teacher to stop the tape.

1. It might snow.
2. Not one of the workers is inside the factory.
3. Some workers are standing near a garbage can.
4. Someone is giving coffee to the workers.
5. Some workers are holding signs.
6. Several people are at the table.
7. They are making a lot of noise.
8. The workers want more money.
9. The workers want more sick days.
10. They all want the strike to end soon.

I. **On Your Own**   Complete this chart. What is the union asking for? What is the company offering? What do you think the agreement will be?

	Union	Company	Agreement
Pay increase	10%		
Sick Days			

LISTENING DISCRIMINATION

J. Listen and Circle   Listen to these sentences from the story. Circle the verb you hear. Listen carefully for singular and plural.

   1. a. is   b. are

   2. a. isn't snowing   b. aren't snowing

   3. a. is wearing   b. are wearing

   4. a. is standing   b. are standing

   5. a. is handing out   b. are handing out

   6. a. is carrying   b. are carrying

   7. a. is sitting   b. are sitting

   8. a. is talking   b. are talking

   9. a. is asking   b. are asking

 10. a. is offering   b. are offering

K. Listen and Write   Listen to these sentences from the story. Write the verb you hear. Some of the verbs are singular, others are plural.

1. _____   6. _____

2. _____   7. _____

3. _____   8. _____

4. _____   9. _____

5. _____   10. _____

L. **Fill In** Complete these sentences from the story with the correct verb.

1. The sky _____ gray and heavy.

2. The workers _____ outside, on strike.

3. Several of them _____ _____ around a garbage can.

4. They _____ _____ their hands over the fire.

5. One worker _____ _____ out coffee.

6. They _____ _____ signs.

7. Six people _____ _____ around the table.

8. The union _____ _____ for a 10% increase in pay.

9. The company _____ _____ only 3%.

10. Each side _____ tired and nervous.

M. **Fill In** Complete these sentences with the correct word from the list below.

it
they   their   them

1. _____'s February.

2. None of _____ are inside the factory.

3. _____'re outside, on stike.

4. Several of _____ are standing around a garbage can.

5. _____'re holding _____ hands over the fire.

6. _____'re carrying signs.

7. Inside, _____'s hot.

8. _____ jackets are off, and _____'re sweating.

N.   **Prepositions**   Complete these sentences with the correct preposition.

1. None of them is _____ the factory.

2. Several of them are standing _____ a garbage can.

3. They're holding their hands _____ the fire.

4. Six people are sitting _____ the table.

5. The union leaders are sitting _____ one side, and the company

   bosses are _____ the other.

6. The union is asking for a 10% increase _____ pay.

7. Today is the fifth day _____ the strike.

8. Everyone hopes there will be an agreement _____ two or three

   days.

CONVERSATION

O.   Listen to the conversation a few times. Then, answer these questions.

       Who is talking?
       Where are they?
       Who is "they" in the sentence, "They're all inside"?
       What does the one worker want?
       What does he ask the other worker?

P.   **Synonyms**   Listen to the conversation again. Write a word that means almost the same as the words below.

       at this moment   _____

       What's going on?   _____

       in a day or two   _____

       Would you like?   _____

Q.   **Complete the Conversation**   The teacher may play the conversation several times.

Worker 1: _____

Worker 2: Not much. They're all inside. They're not telling us anything.

Worker 1: _____

Worker 2: Soon, I hope. It's freezing!

Worker 1: _____

Worker 2: Over there. And get a sign, too.

Worker 1: _____

Worker 2: Yes, thanks.

RETIREMENT

LISTENING COMPREHENSION

A. Discuss these questions with your class.

At what age do people retire? How old are you now? When are you going to retire? What do people do after they retire?

B. **Vocabulary** Talk about the new vocabulary words. If possible, point out the items in the story pictures. Repeat each word after the teacher.

custodian	*fish*
mopping	*during the week*
plans	*in peace and quiet*
patio	*lucky guy*

C. **First Listening** Look at the pictures and listen to the story as many times as you want. After you listen, tell the class any information you remember about the story.

D. **Listen and Choose** Listen to the story again. Check the things that Juan is going to do after he retires.

_____ 1. move to Florida

_____ 2. paint the house

_____ 3. work in the garden

_____ 4. fish

_____ 5. add a patio to the back of the house

_____ 6. visit his family

_____ 7. buy a boat

_____ 8. open a small business

_____ 9. work part-time

E. **Listen and Number**   Listen to these sentences from the story. Write the number of the picture in the correct space.

1. _____   6. _____

2. _____   7. _____

3. _____   8. _____

4. _____   9. _____

5. _____   10. _____

F. **True or False**   Listen to these statements. Write T if the statement is true, F if the statement is false.

1. _____   6. _____

2. _____   7. _____

3. _____   8. _____

4. _____   9. _____

5. _____   10. _____

G. **Word Groups**   Listen to the story again. As you listen, write a few words which you can put in each group.

Time   *Clean*

years   *custodian*

_____   _____

_____   _____

_____   _____

_____   _____

H. **Listen and STOP!** Read these sentences. Then listen to the tape again. When you hear a sentence that means almost the same as each sentence below, tell the teacher to stop the tape.

1. Juan is cleaning the floor.
2. Juan is not going to work again after today.
3. He has to retire.
4. How is he going to keep busy?
5. In December, they're going to see their daughter.
6. Juan doesn't like to fish on the weekends.
7. He might like retirement.
8. His friends from work are entering the building.
9. We're going out together.
10. Come on!

I. **With a Group** Answer these questions about yourself on the lines below. Then talk about your answers in a group.

1. How old are you now?
2. In what year are you going to retire?
3. How old will you be then?
4. Where are you going to live when you retire?
5. What are you going to do when you retire?

1. _____

2. _____

3. _____

4. _____

5. _____

_____

LISTENING DISCRIMINATION

J. **Listen and Circle** Listen to these sentences from the story. Some are in the present continuous tense, others are in the future. Circle the verb you hear.

1. a. is mopping   b. is going to mop

2. a. is doing   b. is going to do

3. a. is painting   b. is going to paint

4. a. isn't thinking   b. isn't going to think

5. a. is adding   b. is going to add

6. a. are flying   b. are going to fly

7. a. is smiling   b. is going to smile

8. a. is fishing   b. is going to fish

9. a. is enjoying   b. is going to enjoy

10. a. are coming   b. are going to come

K. **Listen and Write** Listen to these sentences from the story. Some of the verbs are in the present continuous tense; some are in the future. Write the verb you hear.

1. _____   5. _____

2. _____   6. _____

3. _____   7. _____

4. _____   8. _____

L.   Fill In   Complete these sentences from the story with a verb in the present continuous or the future tense.

1. Juan _____ _____ the front hall of his school.

2. He _____ _____ _____ _____ the house.

3. Juan _____ _____ _____ _____a patio to the back of the

   house.

4. His sons _____ _____ _____ _____ him.

5. He _____ _____ _____ _____ during the week.

6. He _____ _____ _____ _____ in his boat in peace and

   quiet.

7. Juan _____ _____ his mop away.

8. His friends _____ _____ through the front door.

M.   Fill In   Complete these sentences with the correct word from the list below.

        he   his   him

1. _____'s mopping the front hall of _____ school.

2. _____'s sixty-five years old.

3. What's he going to do with all _____ time?

4. _____ isn't thinking about his work.

5. _____ and Luisa have plans.

6. _____ sons are going to help _____ .

7. He's going to sit in _____ boat in peace and quiet.

8. Maybe _____ is going to enjoy retirement.

N. Prepositions Complete these sentences with the correct preposition.

1. Juan is a custodian _____ the Los Altos School System.

2. Forty years _____ mopping, cleaning, fixing.

3. It's Juan's last day _____ work.

4. He isn't thinking _____ his work.

5. What's he going to do _____ all his time?

6. He's going to add a patio _____ the back _____ the house.

7. _____ Christmas, they're going to visit their daughter.

8. No more Saturdays and Sundays _____ all the people and the noise.

9. He's going to sit _____ his boat in peace and quiet.

10. We're taking you _____ B.J.'s Bar.

CONVERSATION

O.   Listen to the conversation a few times. Then, answer these questions.

> How many people are talking?
> Who are they?
> Where are they?
> What is Juan going to do tomorrow?
> Who is the "new man"?
> Is Juan going to visit his friends?

P.   **Synonyms**   Listen to the conversation again. Write a word that means almost the same as the words below.

> Wonderful!   _____
>
> heavy   _____
>
> many   _____
>
> kind   _____
>
> men   _____

Q.   **Complete the Conversation**   The teacher may play the conversation several times.

Charlie: How does it feel, Juan? Your last day of work?

Juan: _____

_____

Pete: Be careful. You're going to get fat.

Juan: _____

_____

Charlie: Did you meet the new man yet?

Pete: Man? He's just a boy.

Juan: _____

Charlie: Are you going to come back and see us?

Juan: _____

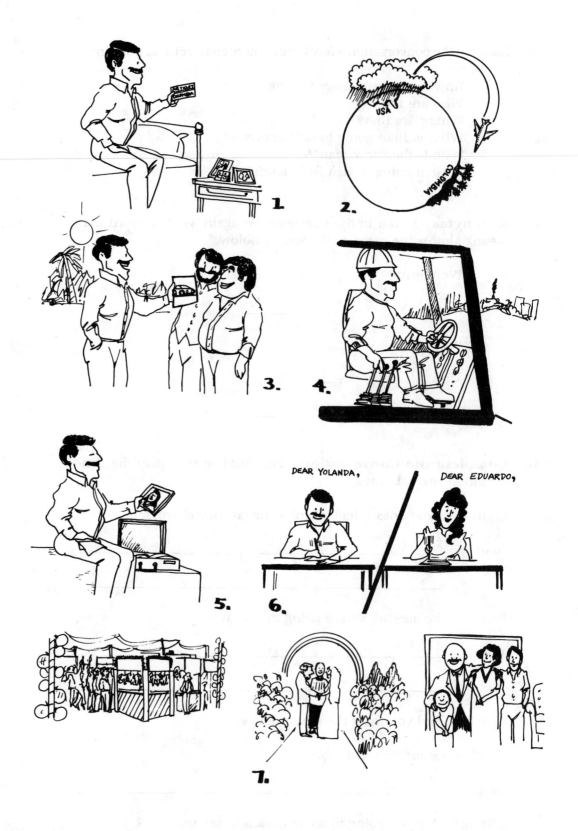

LISTENING COMPREHENSION

A. Discuss these questions with your class.

Some students are refugees. They cannot return to their native countries. Other students are immigrants. They can visit their native countries if they have the time and the money.

Did you ever return to your native country? When? Are you going to visit your native country at some time in the future? What are your plans? How much is an airline ticket from here to your country?

B. **Vocabulary** Talk about the new vocabulary words. If possible, point out the items in the story pictures. Repeat each word after the teacher.

native	*serious*
lonesome	*plans*
packing	*attend*
suitcase	*alone*

C. **First Listening** Look at the pictures and listen to the story as many times as you want. After you listen, tell the class any information you remember about the story.

D. **Listen and Choose** What is Eduardo going to do when he visits Colombia? Check all the things he's going to do in Colombia.

_____ 1. talk with his family about America

_____ 2. work hard

_____ 3. attend a wedding

_____ 4. look for an apartment

_____ 5. visit Yolanda's house

_____ 6. go to a carnival

_____ 7. write to Yolanda

E. **Listen and Number**   Listen to these sentences from the story. Write the number of the picture in the correct space.

1. _____   6. _____

2. _____   7. _____

3. _____   8. _____

4. _____   9. _____

5. _____   10. _____

F. **True or False**   Listen to these statements. Write T if the statement is true, F if the statement is false.

1. _____   6. _____

2. _____   7. _____

3. _____   8. _____

4. _____   9. _____

5. _____   10. _____

G. **Word Groups**   Listen to the story again. As you listen, write a few words which you can put in each group.

Time

three years ago

_____

_____

Places

Cartagena

_____

_____

H.   Listen and STOP!   Read these sentences. Then listen to the tape again. When you hear a sentence that means almost the same as each sentence below, tell the teacher to stop the tape.

1. He's going to arrive in Colombia tomorrow.
2. It's summer in Colombia.
3. What are his family and friends going to think about him?
4. He has lots of photographs in his suitcase.
5. He's going to describe his job.
6. Eduardo and Yolanda attended the same school.
7. They're going to go several places together.
8. They don't know what their feelings are going to be.
9. Are they going to get married?

I.   On Your Own   Eduardo has many plans for his vacation. Use your imagination. You are going to return to your country for a one-month vacation. Write five things that you're going to do.

_____

_____

_____

_____

_____

With a Group   Now, think about a vacation you're planning. Ask one another these questions.

Where are you going to go?
Are you going alone or with family or friends?
When are you going to leave?
How long are you going to stay there?
How are you going to get there?
Who are you going to stay with? or
     Where are you going to stay?
What are you going to do?
When are you going to return?

LISTENING DISCRIMINATION

J.   **Listen and Circle**   Listen to these sentences from the story. Circle the verb you hear.

1. am going to be   is going to be   are going to be

2. am going to leave   is going to leave   are going to leave

3. am going to think   is going to think   are going to think

4. am going to   is going to   are going to
   understand   understand   understand

5. am going to show   is going to show   are going to show

6. am going to tell   is going to tell   are going to tell

7. am going to go   is going to go   are going to go

8. am going to visit   is going to visit   are going to visit

9. am going to return   is going to return   are going to return

10. am going to return   is going to return   are going to return

K.   **Listen and Write**   Listen to these sentences from the story. Write the verb you hear.

1. _____   6. _____

2. _____   7. _____

3. _____   8. _____

4. _____   9. _____

5. _____   10. _____

L. Fill In Complete these sentences from the story with a verb in the future tense.

1. He _____ _____ _____ _____ them

   pictures of America.

2. He _____ _____ _____ _____ them

   how lonesome he feels.

3. Eduardo and Yolanda _____ _____ _____

   _____ a friend's wedding.

4. How _____ he _____ _____ _____ about

   her?

5. Eduardo _____ _____ _____ _____ to

   America in one month.

M. Listen and Write Listen to these questions about the story. Answer with one of the following:

Yes, he is.   Yes, they are.
No, he isn't.   No, they aren't.

1. _____   5. _____

2. _____   6. _____

3. _____   7. _____

4. _____   8. _____

N. Prepositions   Complete these sentences with the correct preposition.

1. Eduardo is looking _____ his airline ticket.

2. Tomorrow he's going to be _____ his family _____ Cartagena.

3. He's going to leave the cold and snow _____ New Jersey _____

   the hot sun _____ his native Colombia.

4. He's bringing lots _____ pictures _____ America.

5. He's looking _____ a picture _____ Yolanda.

6. They've been writing _____ two years.

7. They're going to visit _____ Yolanda's family.

8. How are they going to feel _____ each other?

9. Eduardo is going to return to America _____ one month.

10. Am I going to have a wife _____ my side?

CONVERSATION

O. Listen to the conversation a few times. Then, answer these questions.

>   Who is talking?
>   Where are they?
>   What country are they both from?
>   How long was the other passenger in the United States?
>   How does the other passenger feel about the United States?

P. **Synonyms** Listen to the conversation again. Write a word that means almost the same as the words below.

>   Is it okay with you?   _____
>
>   And you?   _____
>
>   I'm looking forward   _____
>
>   stayed   _____
>
>   I agree   _____

Q. **Complete the Conversation** The teacher may play the conversation several times.

Passenger: _____

Eduardo: No, go ahead.

Passenger: _____

Eduardo: Yes. How about you?

Passenger: _____

Eduardo: I feel the same. I haven't seen my family in three years.

Passenger: _____

_____

Eduardo: I'm only going to be here for a month.

Passenger: _____

YOUNG LOVE

LISTENING COMPREHENSION

A. Discuss these questions with your class.

In your country, at what age do men and women marry? At what age did you (or your parents) get married? In this country, a man often gives a woman an engagement ring when he asks her to marry him. In your country, is this custom the same?

B. **Vocabulary** Talk about the new vocabulary words. If possible, point out the items in the story pictures. Repeat each word after the teacher.

typist	*especially*
continue	*science*
go out	*laboratory technican*
scholarship	*career*

C. **First Listening** Look at the pictures and listen to the story as many times as you want. After you listen, tell the class any information you remember about the story.

D. **Listen and Choose** Robert and Angela have different plans for the future. Who wants to do each of the following? Write R for Robert or A for Angela before each sentence.

_____ 1. go to college

_____ 2. go out with other people

_____ 3. continue the family business

_____ 4. get married in a few months

_____ 5. have four or five children

_____ 6. have one or two children

_____ 7. have a family and a career

_____ 8. be a laboratory technician

E.   Listen and Number   Listen to these sentences from the story. Write the number of the picture in the correct space.

1. _____   6. _____

2. _____   7. _____

3. _____   8. _____

4. _____   9. _____

5. _____   10. _____

F.   True or False   Listen to these statements. Write T if the statement is true, F if the statement is false.

1. _____   6. _____

2. _____   7. _____

3. _____   8. _____

4. _____   9. _____

5. _____   10. _____

G.   Word Groups   Listen to the story again. As you listen, write a few words which you can put in each group.

Work   *Time*

typist   *tomorrow*

_____   _____

_____   _____

_____   _____

_____   _____

H. **Listen and STOP!**   Read these sentences. Then listen to the tape again. When you hear a sentence that means almost the same as each sentence below, tell the teacher to stop the tape.

1. I'm in the 12th grade.
2. Angela and I have a good time.
3. I'm going to say, "Will you marry me?"
4. Angela can be a secretary.
5. We're going to have several children.
6. Someday, it's going to be my shoe store.
7. In school, I do well in science.
8. I'm going to start college in September.
9. I'm going to have a small family.
10. I know Robert very well.

I. **With a Group**   Interview one student who is not married. Ask him or her these questions:

> When are you going to get married?
> Are you going out with anyone special now?
> How many children do you want?
> Are you going to go to college?
> What are you going to study (or be)?

On Your Own   Robert and Angela have many plans for the future. What are your plans? Write a few sentences about your future plans and goals.

_____

_____

_____

_____

LISTENING DISCRIMINATION

J. Listen and Circle   Listen to these sentences from the story. Circle the verb you hear.

1. am   is   are

2. am   is   are

3. am   is   are

4. am   is   are

5. am   is   are

6. am going to take   is going to take   are going to take

7. am going to live   is going to live   are going to live

8. am going to have   is going to have   are going to have

9. am going to say   is going to say   are going to say

10. am going to go   is going to go   are going to go

K. Listen and Write   Listen to these sentences from the story. Write the verb you hear.

1. _____   6. _____

2. _____   7. _____

3. _____   8. _____

4. _____   9. _____

5. _____   10. _____

L. Fill In   Complete these sentences from the story with a form of the verb "to be" or a verb in the future.

1. I _____ Robert.

2. My girlfriend's name _____ Angela.

3. I _____ _____ _____ _____ her to marry me.

4. We _____ _____ _____ _____ in an apartment.

5. Angela and I _____ _____ _____ _____ four or

five children.

6. I _____ _____ _____ _____ the family

business.

7. Robert _____ handsome and kind.

8. I _____ a good student.

9. I _____ _____ _____ _____ a laboratory technician.

10. I _____ _____ _____ _____ out with other boys at

school.

M. Articles Listen to these sentences from the story. Some have the article "a," others do not. If you hear "a," write it on the line. If not, put an "x."

1. I'm _____ senior in high school.

2. Angela is _____ beautiful.

3. I have _____ surprise for her.

4. We can save _____ money for _____ house.

5. I love _____ children.

6. I already have _____ job.

7. Robert is _____ kind.

8. He's _____ fun to be with.

9. I'm going to have _____ small family some day.

10. I know Robert is going to be _____ happy.

N.   Prepositions   Complete these sentences with the correct preposition.

1. I'm a senior _____ high school.

2. I have a surprise _____ her.

3. We're going to live _____ an apartment.

4. She can work _____ an office _____ a year or two.

5. We can save money _____ a house.

6. I have a scholarship _____ college.

7. I'm going to go _____ college _____ the fall.

8. I'm a good student, especially _____ science.

9. I'm going to go out _____ other boys.

10. Robert is going to be happy when I tell him _____ my scholarship.

CONVERSATION

O.   Listen to the conversation a few times. Then, answer these questions.

>   Who is talking?
>   Where are they?
>   What are Robert's ideas about his future?
>   How is he going to have enough money when he is married?
>   What does Robert's father want him to do?

P.   **Synonyms**   Listen to the conversation again. Write a word that means almost the same as the words below.

>   not old enough   _____
>
>   just   _____
>
>   money   _____
>
>   work   _____

Q.   **Complete the Conversation**   The teacher may play the conversation several times.

Robert: _____

Father: What are you going to do?

Robert: _____

Father: Robert, you're too young. You're only eighteen.

Robert: _____

Father: How can you live on your salary from the store?

Robert: _____

Father: What about college?

Robert: _____

DIVORCE

LISTENING COMPREHENSION

A. Discuss these questions with your class.

Do you know anyone who is divorced? Did they have children? What happened to the children? Do they live with their mother or with their father? How often do they see the other parent?

B. **Vocabulary** Talk about the new vocabulary words. If possible, point out the items in the story pictures. Repeat each word after the teacher.

argue	*summer*
anymore	*anytime*
weekend	*together*
far	

C. **First Listening** Look at the pictures and listen to the story as many times as you want. After you listen, tell the class any information you remember about the story.

D. **Listen and Choose** Read the questions below. Then listen to the selection again. Does the story give the answer to any of the questions? Put a check before any questions that the story answers.

_____ 1. Why are Marsha and Ed getting divorced?

_____ 2. Who are the boys going to live with?

_____ 3. How much alimony is Ed going to pay?

_____ 4. How long have Ed and Marsha been having problems?

_____ 5. How often are the boys going to see their father?

E. **Listen and Number**   Listen to these sentences from the story.
Write the number of the picture in the correct space.

1. _____   6. _____

2. _____   7. _____

3. _____   8. _____

4. _____   9. _____

5. _____   10. _____

F. **True or False**   Listen to these statements. Write T if the statement
is true, F if the statement is false.

1. _____   6. _____

2. _____   7. _____

3. _____   8. _____

4. _____   9. _____

5. _____   10. _____

G. **Word Groups**   Listen to the story again. As you listen, write a few
words which you can put in each group.

Upset   *Time*

nervous   _anymore_

_____   _____

_____   _____

_____   _____

H. **Listen and STOP!**   Read these sentences. Then listen to the tape
again. When you hear a sentence that means almost the same as
each sentence below, tell the teacher to stop the tape.

1. Their sons are at the table, too.
2. They're always fighting.
3. Their parents are going to leave each other.

4. The boys are going to stay with their mother.
5. They're not going to leave their friends.
6. Their father is going to leave in a few days.
7. The boys are going to be with their father every other weekend.
8. They want their father to stay.

I. **With a Group**   Talk in your group about a couple you know who got a divorce. Discuss these questions.

1. Who was the couple?
2. How long were they married?
3. Why did they get a divorce?
4. Did they both want the divorce?
5. When couples get a divorce, they usually divide their possessions, such as furniture, cars, and money. Who got which possessions?
6. Where there any children? If yes, how many? Who do they live with? How often do they see their other parent?
7. Is either person remarried?

LISTENING DISCRIMINATION

J. **Listen and Circle**   Listen to these sentences from the story. Circle the verb you hear.

1. a. are sitting   b. are going to sit

2. a. is smoking   b. is going to smoke

3. a. are getting   b. are going to get

4. a. are having   b. are going to have

5. a. are staying   b. are going to stay

6. a. is talking   b. is going to talk

7. a. is leaving   b. is going to leave

8. a. is not moving   b. is not going to move

9. a. are being   b. are going to be

10. a. is being   b. is going to be

K. Listen and Write   Listen to these sentences from the story. Write the verb you hear.

1. _____   6. _____

2. _____   7. _____

3. _____   8. _____

4. _____   9. _____

5. _____   10. _____

L. Fill In   Complete these sentences from the story with the correct verb.

1. Marsha and Ed Gibson _____ _____ at the kitchen table.

2. Marsha's eyes _____ red.

3. Their parents _____ happy together.

4. Tony and George know that their parents _____ _____ problems.

5. Their parents _____ _____ _____ _____ a divorce.

6. They _____ _____ _____ _____ together as a family anymore.

7. The boys _____ _____ _____ _____ with their mother.

8. They _____ _____ _____ _____ to the same school.

9. Their father _____ _____ _____ _____ the house this weekend.

10. Two weekends a month, they _____ _____ _____ _____ with him.

M. **Fill In** Complete these sentences with the correct word from the list below.

> they   their   them

1. _____ children are sitting with _____ .

2. Tony and George know that _____ parents are having

    problems.

3. _____ mom and dad aren't happy together anymore.

4. _____'re going to get a divorce.

5. _____ mother is talking first.

6. She loves _____ and _____ father loves _____ ,

    too.

7. _____'re going to stay in the same house.

8. _____'re going to be with all _____ friends.

N. **Prepositions** Complete these sentences with the correct preposition.

1. Marsha and Ed Gibson are sitting _____ the kitchen table.

2. Their children are sitting _____ them.

3. It has nothing to do _____ the boys.

4. The boys are going to live _____ her.

5. They're going to stay _____ the same house.

6. Their father is going to be _____ the next town.

7. Two weekends a month, the boys are going to stay _____ him.

8. They're going to be _____ him one month _____ the summer-

    time.

CONVERSATION

O.   Listen to the conversation a few times. Then, answer these questions.

   Who's talking?
   Where are they?
   Where are they going now?
   What are they going to do tomorrow?

P.   **Synonyms**   Listen to the conversation again. Write a word that means almost the same as the words below.

   children   _____

   of course   _____

   Saturday and Sunday   _____

   Do you want   _____

Q. Complete the Conversation The teacher may play the conversation several times.

Father: Come on, kids, in the car. Did you eat lunch yet?

Son: _____

Father: Let's go to McDonald's.

Son: _____

Father: Sure. Anything you want.

Son: _____

Father: Would you like to go to a baseball game?

Son: _____

Father: The Yankees and the Angels. And I have three tickets for

tomorrow's game.

III.
Present Tense

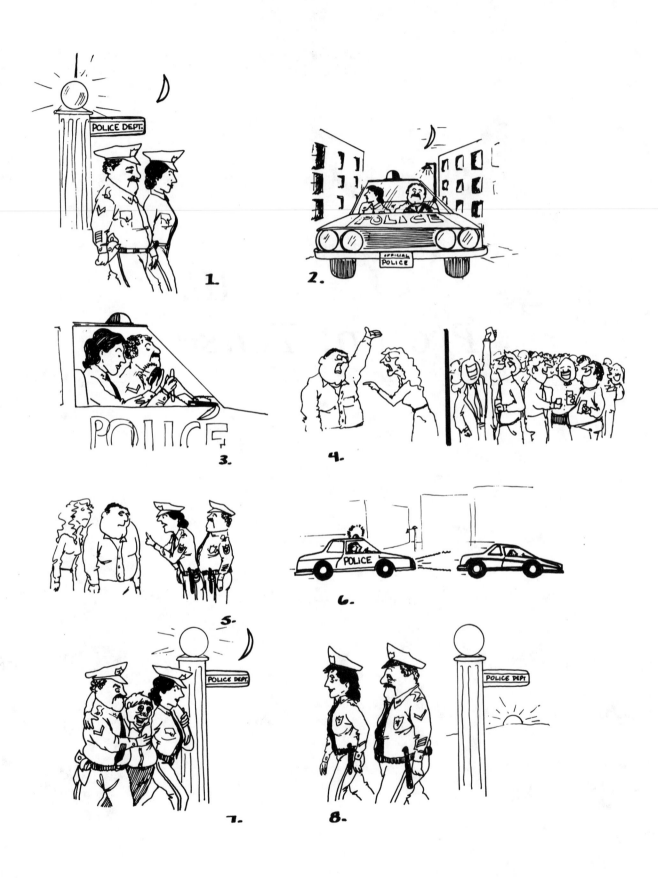

TWO OFFICERS

LISTENING COMPREHENSION

A. Discuss these questions with your class.

Police officers have a busy and dangerous job. What are some of the common problems that police officers take care of at night?

B. Vocabulary Talk about the new vocabulary words. If possible, point out the items in the story pictures. Repeat each word after the teacher.

report	*common*
patrol	*quiet down*
robbery	*arrest*
strangers	*speeding*

C. First Listening Look at the pictures and listen to the story again, as many times as you want. After you listen, tell the class any information you remember about the story.

D. Listen and Choose Pappas and Frezza are busy on the night shift. Listen to the tape again and check the problems that the story talks about.

_____ 1. fires

_____ 2. family fights

_____ 3. drunk drivers

_____ 4. accidents

_____ 5. robberies

_____ 6. parking tickets

_____ 7. drug sales

_____ 8. loud parties

E. **Listen and Number**   Listen to these sentences from the story. Write the number of the picture in the correct space.

1. _____   6. _____

2. _____   7. _____

3. _____   8. _____

4. _____   9. _____

5. _____   10. _____

F. **True or False**   Listen to these statements. Write T if the statement is true, F if the statement is false.

1. _____   6. _____

2. _____   7. _____

3. _____   8. _____

4. _____   9. _____

5. _____   10. _____

G. **Word Groups**   Listen to the story again. As you listen, write a few words which you can put in each group.

Car

*drives.*_____

_____

_____

_____

Police

*officer*_____

_____

_____

_____

H. **Listen and STOP!** Read these sentences. Then listen to the tape again. When you hear a sentence that means almost the same as each sentence below, tell the teacher to stop the tape.

1. Officer Pappas arrives at work at 11:00.
2. He works with a woman.
3. Frezza checks the buildings carefully.
4. They receive information from the police radio.
5. There is too much noise at some parties.
6. Most people stop the noise or fighting when the officers arrive.
7. Pappas and Frezza look for drunk drivers.
8. They arrest drunk drivers.
9. They drive many miles every night.
10. They go home at 7:00 a.m.

I. **With a Group**

A. On television, there are many shows about police and their work. Do you watch any of these shows? Write the names of two police programs.

_____

_____

Write the names of two other shows you watch frequently.

_____

_____

Compare your lists with the lists made by other students in the group. Are any of the shows popular with several students?

B. Did you ever call the police? What was the problem? Tell your group what happened.

LISTENING DISCRIMINATION

J. **Listen and Circle** Listen to these sentences from the story. Circle the verb you hear.

1. a. report   b. reports

2. a. works   b. works

3. a. listen   b. listens

4. a. are   b. is

5. a. make   b. makes

6. a. watch   b. watches

7. a. turn on   b. turns on

8. a. stop   b. stops

9. a. arrest   b. arrests

10. a. bring   b. brings

K. **Listen and Write** Listen to these sentences from the story. Write the verb you hear.

1. _____   6. _____

2. _____   7. _____

3. _____   8. _____

4. _____   9. _____

5. _____   10. _____

L. **Fill In**   Complete these sentences from the story with a verb in the present tense.

   1. Officer Pappas _____ to the police station at 11 p.m.

   2. He _____ the night shift.

   3. Pappas and Frezza _____ the east side of town.

   4. Pappas _____ slowly up and down the streets.

   5. Frezza _____ carefully at the stores and houses.

   6. Pappas and Frezza _____ to the police radio.

   7. They _____ for drunk drivers.

   8. Pappas _____ on the flashing red lights.

   9. If the driver is drunk, they _____ him.

   10. Pappas and Frezza _____ home at 7 a.m.

M. **Singular or Plural**   Listen to these sentences. Do you hear a singular or plural noun? Circle the word you hear.

   1. shift   shifts

   2. partner   partners

   3. robbery   robberies

   4. house   houses

   5. fight   fights

   6. arrest   arrests

   7. driver   drivers

   8. driver   drivers

   9. mile   miles

   10. ticket   tickets

N.   Prepositions   Complete these sentences with the correct preposition.

1. Officer Pappas reports _____ the police station _____ 11 p.m.

2. There are many robberies _____ night.

3. Frezza looks carefully _____ the stores and houses.

4. She watches _____ open windows.

5. As they drive, the two officers watch _____ drunk drivers.

6. They bring him _____ the police station.

7. Most nights, Pappas and Frezza drive _____ 150 miles.

8. _____ 7:00 a.m., they go home.

CONVERSATION

O.   Listen to the conversation a few times. Then, answer these questions.

Who is talking?
Where are they?
Why are the police at this house?
What is the reason for the party?
What is Mr. White going to do?

P.   **Synonyms**   Listen to the conversation again. Write a word that means almost the same as the words below.

We want   _____

three or four   _____

unhappy   _____

know   _____

Q.   **Complete the Conversation**   The teacher may play the conversation several times.

Mr. White: _____

Officer: We'd like to speak to the owner of this house.

Mr. White: _____

Officer: _____

Mr. White: It's my daughter's graduation party. I didn't realize the

music was so loud.

Officer: _____

Mr. White: I'm sorry. They'll quiet down.

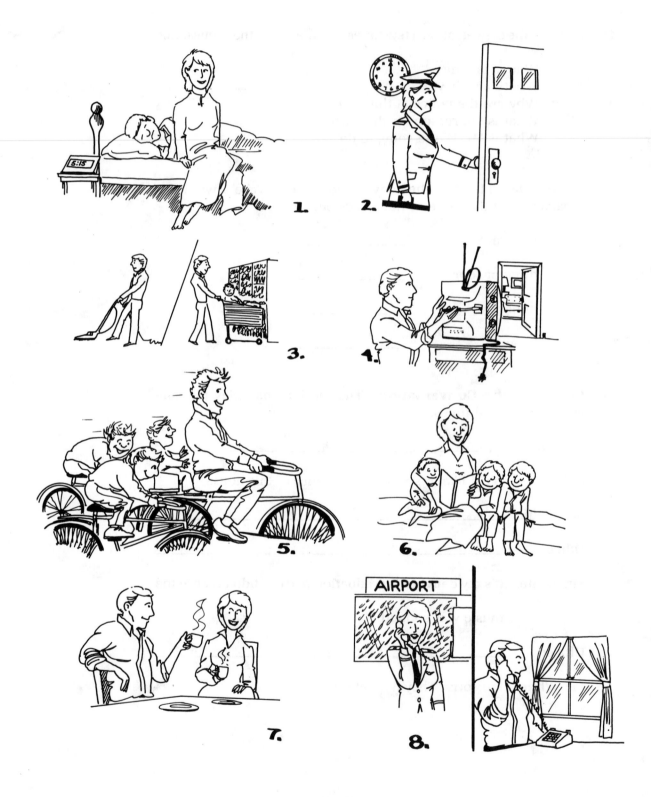

ANA AND PETER

LISTENING COMPREHENSION

A. Discuss these questions with your class.

What is a housewife? A househusband? In your house, who cooks, shops, does the laundry, cleans, etc.? Is it only one person or does everyone help?

B. **Vocabulary**   Talk about the new vocabulary words. If possible, point out the items in the story pictures. Repeat each word after the teacher.

pilot	*spend time*
shuttle	*nap*
flight	*weather*
still	*misses*

C. **First Listening**   Look at the pictures and listen to the story as many times as you want. After you listen, tell the class any information you remember about the story.

D. **Listen and Choose**   Ana and Peter have busy lives. Who does each of the following in their family? Write A for Ana or P for Peter.

_____ 1. flies the daily shuttle from New York to Boston

_____ 2. gets the chidren ready for school

_____ 3. shops for the food

_____ 4. has a small business at home

_____ 5. helps the children with their homework

_____ 6. reads to the children

_____ 7. leaves the house early in the morning

_____ 8. does the laundry

_____ 9. gets the children ready for bed

_____ 10. cleans the house

E.   Listen and Number   Listen to these sentences from the story. Write the number of the picture in the correct space.

1. _____   6. _____

2. _____   7. _____

3. _____   8. _____

4. _____   9. _____

5. _____   10. _____

F.   True or False   Listen to these statements. Write T if the statement is true, F if the statement is false.

1. _____   6. _____

2. _____   7. _____

3. _____   8. _____

4. _____   9. _____

5. _____   10. _____

G.   Word Groups   Listen to the story again. As you listen, write a few words which you can put in each group.

Pilot   *Family*

flies   *husband*

_____   _____

_____   _____

_____   _____

H. **Listen and STOP!**   Read these sentences. Then listen to the tape again. When you hear a sentence that means almost the same as each sentence below, tell the teacher to stop the tape.

1. Ana gets up early in the morning.
2. When she goes to work, everyone is in bed.
3. Peter enjoys being home.
4. He thinks many fathers don't see their children enough.
5. All morning, he does housework.
6. After school, they have fun outside.
7. After they eat, Ana spends time with the children.
8. Sometimes, the children are in bed when Ana gets home.
9. The plane isn't on time.
10. Peter understands how Ana feels about her job.

I. **With a Group**   Ana and Peter have busy lives. A student usually has a busy life, too. Many students are working or have families. On the lines below, list your daily routine. Then, compare your list with lists made by other people in your group. Check the things that all or most of you do every day. If you do something that is different from everyone else, circle it.

Time   *Activity*

_____   _____

_____   _____

_____   _____

_____   _____

_____   _____

_____   _____

_____   _____

_____   _____

_____   _____

_____   _____

LISTENING DISCRIMINATION

J.   Listen and Circle   Listen to these sentences from the story. Circle the verb you hear.

1. a. get up   b. gets up

2. a. leave   b. leaves

3. a. stay   b. stays

4. a. enjoy   b. enjoys

5. a. take   b. takes

6. a. play   b. plays

7. a. read   b. reads

8. a. have   b. has

9. a. don't see   b. doesn't see

10. a. like   b. likes

K.   Listen and Circle   You will hear two sentences. Decide if they are the same or different. Circle "same" or "different."

1. same	different	6. same	different
2. same	different	7. same	different
3. same	different	8. same	different
4. same	different	9. same	different
5. same	different	10. same	different

L.   Listen and Write   Listen to these sentences from the story. Write the verb you hear.

1. _____   6. _____

2. _____   7. _____

3. _____   8. _____

4. _____   9. _____

5. _____   10. _____

M.   Fill In   Complete these sentences from the story with the correct verb.

1. Ana _____ at 5:15 four mornings a week.

2. Ana _____ the daily shuttle from New York to Boston.

3. Peter _____ home with the children.

4. In the morning, he _____ and _____ .

5. When the youngest _____ a nap, he _____ TV sets.

6. When the children come home from school, they _____

   bike rides or _____ outside.

7. After dinner, Ana _____ with the children.

8. When the children are in bed, Peter and Ana _____ some

   time to themselves.

9. Some days, Ana _____ _____ home until late.

10. Peter _____ Ana when she isn't home at night.

N.   Prepositions   Complete these sentences with the correct preposition.

1. Ana gets up _____ 5:15 a.m.

2. She leaves her husband and children _____ 6:00 a.m.

3. She flies the daily shuttle _____ New York _____ Boston.

4. Peter stays home _____ the children.

5. He says that most fathers don't spend enough time _____ their

children.

6. When the children come home _____ school, they play outside.

7. He has a small business _____ home.

8. After dinner, she plays _____ them and reads _____ them.

9. It's eight o'clock and Ana is still _____ Boston.

10. Peter will stay up and wait _____ her.

CONVERSATION

O.   Listen to the conversation a few times. Then, answer these questions.

  Who is talking?
  Where are they?
  What does the boy want to do?
  What are they going to make?
  Then what are they going to do?

P.   **Synonyms**   Listen to the conversation again. Write a word that means almost the same as the words below.

  When   _____

  returning   _____

  not go to bed   _____

  take out   _____

  After that   _____

Q.   **Complete the Conversation**   The teacher may play the conversation several times.

Son: _____

Father: She's going to be late.

Son: _____

Father: No. I don't know what time she's going to be home. Let's

  make some popcorn.

Son: _____

Father: You can get out the popcorn. I'll put it in the popcorn

  popper.

Son: _____

Father: Then, you can go to bed.

1.

2.

3.

4.

5.

6.

7.

8.

9.

GOOD HEALTH

LISTENING COMPREHENSION

A. Discuss these questions with your class.

What is good health? Are you in good health? Do you exercise? smoke? drink? use a lot of salt?

B. **Vocabulary** Talk about the new vocabulary words. If possible, point out the items in the story pictures. Repeat each word after the teacher.

except	*intensive care unit*
shortness of breath	*decaffeinated*
dizzy	*slow down*
collapsed	*increase*

C. **First Listening** Look at the pictures and listen to the story as many times as you want. After you listen, tell the class any information you remember about the story.

D. **Listen and Choose** Leonid is trying to follow the doctor's orders. Check those things that he is trying to do.

_____ 1. lose weight

_____ 2. walk a mile in the morning

_____ 3. eat steak

_____ 4. work more than seven hours a day

_____ 5. eat more vegetables

_____ 6. slow down at the office

_____ 7. eat eggs for breakfast

_____ 8. drink decaffeinated coffee

_____ 9. smoke

_____10. exercise at a local health club

E.   Listen and Number   Listen to these sentences from the story. Write the number of the picture in the correct space.

1. _____	6. _____
2. _____	7. _____
3. _____	8. _____
4. _____	9. _____
5. _____	10. _____

F.   True or False   Listen to these statements. Write T if the statement is true, F if the statement is false.

1. _____	6. _____
2. _____	7. _____
3. _____	8. _____
4. _____	9. _____
5. _____	10. _____

G.   Word Groups   Listen to the story again. As you listen, write a few words which you can put in each group.

Health

pains _____

_____

_____

_____

Food

French fries _____

_____

_____

_____

_____   _____

_____   _____

H. **Listen and STOP!**   Read these sentences. Then listen to the tape again. When you hear a sentence that means almost the same as each sentence below, tell the teacher to stop the tape.

1. Leonid had a birthday last week.
2. Leonid is married and has two girls.
3. He's rich, but money can't buy health.
4. One day Leonid had some trouble breathing.
5. The doctor told Leonid what he could and couldn't do.
6. Leonid can't have two martinis before dinner anymore.
7. He can't drink coffee with caffeine.
8. Leonid doesn't like vegetables.
9. Each month, he can work a little longer at the office.
10. Leonid doesn't understand why this happened to him.

I. **With a Group**   List three kinds of exercise that you like. Next to each, write the number of times each week that you do that kind of exercise.

Exercise   *Time*

_____   _____

_____   _____

_____   _____

Discuss your list with your group. Who does the most exercise? Does anyone go to a health club or exercise class? Does anyone play a team sport regularly? Does anyone use special equipment?

LISTENING DISCRIMINATION

J. Listen and Circle   You will hear two sentences. Decide if they are the same or different. Circle "same" or "different."

1. same   different   6. same   different

2. same   different   7. same   different

3. same   different   8. same   different

4. same   different   9. same   different

5. same   different   10. same   different

K. Listen and Write   Listen to these sentences from the story. Write the verb you hear. All of the verbs are in the present tense.

1. _____   6. _____

2. _____   7. _____

3. _____   8. _____

4. _____   9. _____

5. _____   10. _____

L. Listen and Write   Listen to these sentences from the story. Write the complete verb you hear. Listen for "has to," "can," or "can't."

1. _____   6. _____

2. _____   7. _____

3. _____   8. _____

4. _____   9. _____

5. _____   10. _____

M. Listen to these questions about the story. Answer with "Yes, he can" or "No, he can't."

1. _____

2. _____

3. _____

4. _____

5. _____

6. _____

7. _____

8. _____

9. _____

10. _____

N. **Prepositions** Complete these sentences with the correct preposition.

1. He lives _____ a beautiful home _____ his wife and two daughters.

2. He remembers the terrible pains _____ his chest.

3. _____ two weeks he lay _____ the intensive care unit _____ the hospital.

4. Leonid got his orders _____ the doctor.

5. He dreams _____ steak.

6. Leonid has to slow down _____ the office.

7. He has to exercise _____ a local health club.

8. He misses the excitement _____ the office.

9. How did this happen _____ him?

CONVERSATION

O. Listen to the conversation a few times. Then, answer these questions.

Who is talking?
Where are they?
How is Leonid's heart?
How many pounds did he lose?
What does Leonid miss?
How many hours does Leonid want to work?

P. **Synonyms** Listen to the conversation again. Write a word that means almost the same as the words below.

healthy   _____

you lost   _____

don't like   _____

continue   _____

one more   _____

Q. **Complete the Conversation** The teacher may play the conversation several times.

Doctor: You can put your shirt back on. Your heart sounds strong.

Leonid: _____

_____

Doctor: And you're down five more pounds.

Leonid: _____

_____

Doctor: Stay with the diet.

Leonid: _____

_____

Doctor: The caffeine is no good for you.

Leonid: _____

_____

Doctor: Yes. Try it and see how you feel. If you're tired, go back to

five.

LISTENING COMPREHENSION

A. Discuss these questions with your class.

In your country, what numbers are lucky? What numbers are unlucky? What are some other things that bring bad luck?

B. **Vocabulary** Talk about the new vocabulary words. If possible, point out the items in the story pictures. Repeat each word after the teacher.

alarm   wet
announcer   ignition
knocks   gas gauge
spills   empty

C. **First Listening** Look at the pictures and listen to the story again, as many times as you want. After you listen, tell the class any information you remember about the story.

D. **Listen and Choose** Friday the 13th is an unlucky day for Hiro. Check the unlucky things that happen to him.

_____ 1. He has no gas in his car.

_____ 2. He can't find his clothes.

_____ 3. He spills the orange juice.

_____ 4. He can't find his keys.

_____ 5. He can't find his umbrella.

_____ 6. The refrigerator isn't working.

_____ 7. His car seat is all wet.

E. Listen and Number   Listen to these sentences from the story. Write the number of the picture in the correct space.

1. _____   6. _____

2. _____   7. _____

3. _____   8. _____

4. _____   9. _____

5. _____   10. _____

F. True or False   Listen to these statements. Write T if the statement is true, F if the statement is false.

1. _____   6. _____

2. _____   7. _____

3. _____   8. _____

4. _____   9. _____

5. _____   10. _____

G. Word Groups   Listen to the story again. As you listen, write a few words which you can put in each group.

House   *Car*

*kitchen*_____   *keys*_____

_____   _____

_____   _____

_____   _____

_____

H. **Listen and STOP!**   Read these sentences. Then listen to the tape again. When you hear a sentence that means almost the same as each sentence below, tell the teacher to stop the tape.

   1. Hiro puts on his clothes.
   2. He can't find the orange juice.
   3. The milk goes all over his clothes.
   4. He can't find his car keys.
   5. The window was open last night.
   6. The engine does the same thing again.
   7. He has no gas in his car.
   8. Hiro returns to the house.
   9. He goes to bed again.

I. **With a Group**   In every country, different numbers, animals, and actions are lucky or unlucky.

List three things that are lucky in your country.

1. _____

2. _____

3. _____

List three things that are unlucky in your country.

1. _____

2. _____

3. _____

Discuss your lists with the other students in your group.
Are you a lucky person or an unlucky person? Tell the group about a lucky or an unlucky experience you had in your life.

LISTENING DISCRIMINATION

J. Listen and Circle   You will hear two sentences. Decide if they are the same or different. Circle "same" or "different."

1. same	different	6. same	different
2. same	different	7. same	different
3. same	different	8. same	different
4. same	different	9. same	different
5. same	different	10. same	different

K. Listen and Write   Listen to these sentences from the story. Write the verb you hear.

1. _____   6. _____

2. _____   7. _____

3. _____   8. _____

4. _____   9. _____

5. _____   10. _____

L. Fill In   Complete these sentences from the story with a verb in the present tense.

1. Hiro hears his alarm clock and _____ on his radio.

2. He _____ the refrigerator.

3. He _____ a carton of milk off the shelf.

4. The milk _____ on his pants and shoes.

5. Hiro _____ up the mess.

6. Hiro _____ the key in the ignition and _____ it.

7. The engine _____ , then _____ .

8. He tries again, but the same thing _____ .

9. Hiro _____ his car and goes back in the house.

10. He _____ off his clothes and _____ back into bed.

M. Articles Read these sentences from the story. Is "the" needed? Complete each sentence with "the" or "x" (if no article is needed).

1. Hiro turns on _____ radio.

2. It's _____ Friday, _____ 13th.

3. Hiro dresses and goes into _____ kitchen.

4. Hiro looks in _____ back of _____ refrigerator.

5. The milk spills on his pants and _____ shoes.

6. By now, he's late for _____ work.

7. He didn't close _____ window last night.

8. He puts _____ key in _____ ignition.

9. It's on _____ empty.

10. Hiro leaves his car and goes back in _____ house.

N. Prepositions Complete these sentences with the correct preposition.

1. Hiro goes _____ the kitchen.

2. Hiro looks _____ the back _____ the refrigerator.

3. He knocks a carton _____ milk _____ the shelf.

4. The milk spills _____ his pants.

5. There they are, _____ the top shelf.

6. He runs _____ the rain _____ his car.

7. He goes back _____ the house.

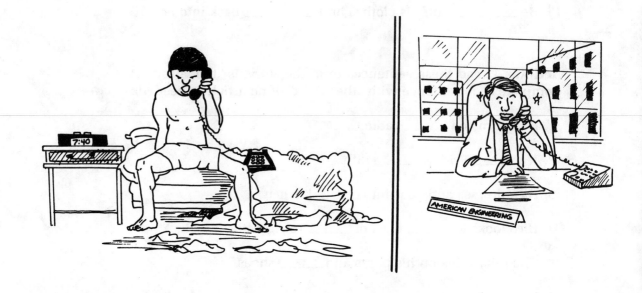

CONVERSATION

O. Listen to the conversation a few times. Then, answer these questions.

Who is speaking?
Where are they?
Is John the boss or are John and Hiro co-workers?
What's the matter with Hiro?
Is that the real reason that Hiro is staying home?
What does John ask Hiro about the office?

P. Synonyms   Listen to the conversation again. Write a word that means almost the same as the words below.

        I feel sick.   _____

        I don't know.   _____

        very bad   _____

        relax   _____

        stay   _____

Q. Complete the Conversation   The teacher may play the conversation several times.

John: American Engineering. John Tandy speaking.

Hiro: _____

John: Hiro! What's the problem? You're not at your desk.

Hiro: _____

John: What's the matter?

Hiro: _____

        _____

John: Just take it easy. I'll tell the boss. Is there anything here you

        need me to do?

Hiro: _____

John: Okay. Take care.

IV.
Past Tense

LISTENING COMPREHENSION

A. Discuss these questions with your class.

Were you or a friend ever robbed? Tell what happened. What did the person steal? Did you call the police? What did they do?

B. **Vocabulary** Talk about the new vocabulary words. If possible, point out the items in the story pictures. Repeat each word after the teacher.

camera	*was stealing*
focused	*robbery*
film	*arrested*
scream	*jail*

C. **First Listening** Look at the pictures and listen to the story as many times as you want. After you listen, tell the class any information you remember about the story.

D. **Listen and Order** Listen to the story again. Then, put these statements in order.

_____Sally took three pictures of the man.

_____Sally decided to take a picture of the children.

_____She heard a scream.

_____The police arrested the man.

_____The Wilsons went to the park.

_____A man was stealing a woman's purse.

_____One of Sally's photographs was in the newspaper.

_____She gave the film to the police.

E. **Listen and Number** Listen to these sentences from the story. Write the number of the picture in the correct space.

    1. _____   6. _____

    2. _____   7. _____

    3. _____   8. _____

    4. _____   9. _____

    5. _____   10. _____

F. **True or False** Listen to these statements. Write T if the statement is true, F if the statement is false.

    1. _____   6. _____

    2. _____   7. _____

    3. _____   8. _____

    4. _____   9. _____

    5. _____   10. _____

G. **Word Groups** Listen to the story again. As you listen, write a few words which you can put in each group.

Camera   *Robbery*

picture _____   *stealing* _____

_____   _____

_____   _____

_____   _____

H. Listen and STOP!   Read these sentences. Then listen to the tape again. When you hear a sentence that means almost the same as each sentence below, tell the teacher to stop the tape.

1. Jim and Sally relaxed.
2. Sally picked up her camera.
3. Someone shouted.
4. A man was taking a woman's pocketbook.
5. He was coming toward her.
6. Sally's photograph was on the front page.
7. Soon, the police knew who the man was.
8. The man is in prison.

I. With a Group   Complete this information about a robbery. Tell about yourself, someone in your family, or someone you know. Then, talk about the information in a group. Tell your stories to each other. Ask questions to find our more information.

1. Who was robbed?

   I (or my _____) was robbed.

2. Where was the robbery?

   It was _____ .

3. When was the robbery?

   It was _____ .

4. What did the robber take?

   He (she) took _____ .

5. Did you (he, she) call the police?

   Yes, _____ did. or No, _____ didn't.

6. What did the police do?

   They _____ .

7. Did they ever arrest the robber?

   Yes, they did.   or   No, they didn't.

LISTENING DISCRIMINATION

J. **Listen and Circle**   You will hear two sentences. Decide if they are
the same or different. Circle "same" or "different."

1. same   different   6. same   different

2. same   different   7. same   different

3. same   different   8. same   different

4. same   different   9. same   different

5. same   different   10. same   different

K. **Listen and Write**   You will hear a statement in the past tense.
Write the verb you hear.

1. _____   6. _____

2. _____   7. _____

3. _____   8. _____

4. _____   9. _____

5. _____   10. _____

L. **Fill In**   Complete these sentences from the story with a verb in the
past tense.

1. Last month, the Wilsons _____ to Green Trees Park.

2. Jim and Sally _____ under the trees.

3. She _____ her camera.

4. Then, she _____ a scream.

5. Sally _____ up.

6. Sally _____ fast.

7. When the police _____ , she _____ them the
film.

8. One of Sally's photographs _____ in the newspaper.

9. In a few hours, the police _____ the man's name.

10. They went to his house and _____ him.

M. Complete these sentences with the correct word from the list below.

she her
he   his him
they   them

1. _____ took _____ camera.

2. She walked over to _____ .

3. She focused _____ camera.

4. Then, _____ heard a scream.

5. _____ was running in _____ direction.

6. When the police came, she gave _____ the film.

7. _____ went to _____ house and arrested

_____ .

N. **Prepositions** Complete these sentences with the correct preposition.

1. The Wilsons went _____ Green Trees Park.

2. Jim and Sally sat _____ the trees.

3. Sally looked _____ .

4. He was running _____ her direction.

5. She took three pictures _____ the man.

6. The next day, one _____ Sally's photographs was _____ the

newspaper.

7. _____ it was the story _____ the robbery.

8. The man is now serving three months _____ jail.

CONVERSATION

O. Listen to the conversation a few times. Then, answer these questions.

Who is talking?
Where is each person?
Who called the police?
What did she tell them?
Where is the man now?
How long is he going to be there?
How many times did the policeman thank Sally?

P. **Synonyms** Listen to the conversation again. Write a word that means almost the same as the words below.

took him to jail _____

quickly _____

photograph _____

needed _____

Don't mention it. _____

Q. **Complete the Conversation** The teacher may play the conversation several times.

Sally: _____

Policeman: Mrs. Wilson, Officer Brown.

Sally: _____

Policeman: We arrested him today.

Sally: _____

Policeman: One of his neighbors called. She saw his picture in the

newspaper.

Sally: _____

Policeman: In jail. He's going to be there for three months. We

want to thank you for your help.

Sally: _____

Policeman: And those pictures gave us the man we wanted. Thank

you again.

Sally: _____

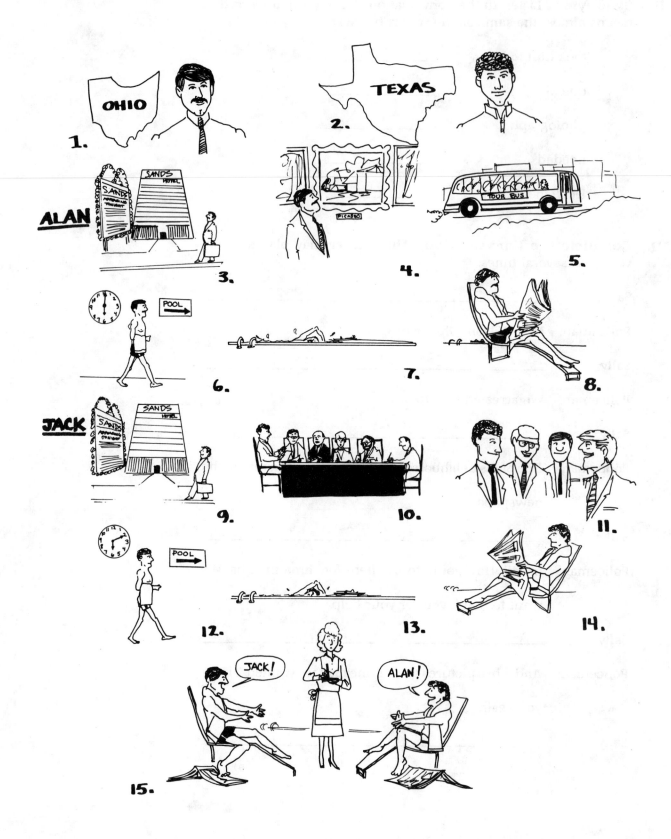

TWO BROTHERS

LISTENING COMPREHENSION

A. Discuss these questions with your class.

Do you have a brother or a sister who lives in the United States? What state does he or she live in? How often do you see him or her?

B. **Vocabulary** Talk about the new vocabulary words. If possible, point out the items in the story pictures. Repeat each word after the teacher.

went sightseeing   meeting
bathing suit   waitress
conference

C. **First Listening** Look at the pictures and listen to the story again, as many times as you want. After you listen, tell the class any information you remember about the story.

D. **Listen and Choose** Read the statements below. Which are about Alan? Which are about Jack? Write A for Alan, J for Jack, AJ for both Alan and Jack.

1. _____He went to a lot of meetings.

2. _____He visited an art museum.

3. _____He ordered a martini.

4. _____He is staying at the Sands Hotel.

5. _____He lives in Ohio.

6. _____He got back to the hotel at 6:00.

7. _____He looked at his brother in surprise.

8. _____He swam for a few minutes.

145

E.   **Listen and Number**   Listen to these sentences from the story. Write the number of the picture in the correct space.

1. _____   6. _____

2. _____   7. _____

3. _____   8. _____

4. _____   9. _____

5. _____   10. _____

F.   **True or False**   Listen to these statements. Write T if the statement is true, F if the statement is false.

1. _____   6. _____

2. _____   7. _____

3. _____   8. _____

4. _____   9. _____

5. _____   10. _____

G.   **Word Groups**   Listen to the story again. As you listen, write a few words which you can put in each group.

Vacation   *Business*

sightseeing   *meetings*

_____   _____

_____   _____

_____   _____

H. **Listen and STOP!** Read these sentences. Then listen to the tape again. When you hear a sentence that means almost the same as each sentence below, tell your teacher to stop the tape.

1. They see each other very little.
2. Alan is relaxing in California.
3. He went to a museum.
4. He returned at 6:00.
5. He was in the pool for a little while.
6. Jack is in California on business.
7. He sat and talked with many people.
8. He changed his clothes.
9. The waitress said, "What do you want?"
10. The brothers saw each other.

I. **With a Group** Sit with one or two students. Ask each one the questions below. Then, complete the chart about yourself and your classmates.

1. Do you have a brother or sister or other relative in the United States?
2. Where does he or she live?
3. How often do you see him or her?

	Relative	State/City	How often
Alan	*Jack*		*maybe once a year*

LISTENING DISCRIMINATION

J.   Listen and Circle   Listen to these sentences from the story. Circle the verb you hear.

1.	aren't seeing	don't see	didn't see
2.	is living	lives	lived
3.	is visiting	visits	visited
4.	is getting	gets	got
5.	is sitting	sits	sat
6.	is staying	stays	stayed
7.	is having	has	had
8.	is asking	asks	asked
9.	is looking	looks	looked
10.		can't believe	couldn't believe

K.   Listen and Write   Listen to these sentences from the story. Write the verb you hear. All the verbs are in the past tense.

1. _____   6. _____

2. _____   7. _____

3. _____   8. _____

4. _____   9. _____

5. _____   10. _____

L   Fill In   Complete these sentences from the story with a verb in the past tense.

1. This morning, Alan _____ an art museum.

2. He _____ back to the hotel at 6:00.

3. Alan _____ in the pool for a few minutes.

4. He _____ up a newspaper.

5. This morning, Jack _____ two meetings.

6. He _____ his bathing suit.

7. A waitress _____ by.

8. They _____ at each other in surprise.

M. Complete these sentences with the correct word from the list below.

> he   his   him
> they   their

1. _____ visited an art museum.

2. He put on _____ bathing suit.

3. _____ began to read _____ newspaper.

4. _____ company sent _____ to a conference.

5. This morning, _____ had two meetings.

6. _____ put down _____ newspapers at the same time.

7. Then, _____ looked at each other in surprise.

N. Prepositions Complete these sentences with the correct preposition.

1. Alan is_____ vacation _____ California.

2. He is staying _____ the Sands Hotel _____ San Francisco.

3. He got back _____ the hotel _____ 6:00.

4. He swam _____ a few minutes.

5. He sat down _____ a chair _____ the side _____ the pool.

6. Jack's company sent him _____ a conference there.

7. They looked _____ each other _____ surprise.

CONVERSATION

O. Listen to the conversation a few times. Then, answer these questions.

> Who is talking?
> Where are they?
> How long is Alan in California for?
> What are they going to do tonight?
> Where are they going to meet each other?

P. **Synonyms** Listen to the conversation again. Write a word that means almost the same as the words below.

I'm so surprised. _____

three or four _____

I'm not doing anything. _____

Why don't we _____

supper _____

Q. **Complete the Conversation** The teacher may play the conversation several times.

A: _____

J: Alan!

A: _____

J: I didn't know you were here!

A: _____

J: You look great!

A: _____

J: I'm here on business. I'm looking at some new cameras for my

company. How about you?

A: _____

J: I just can't believe it! Meeting you here in California!

A: _____

J: I'm free. How about you?

A: _____

J: Good idea. I'll meet you in the lobby at 7:00.

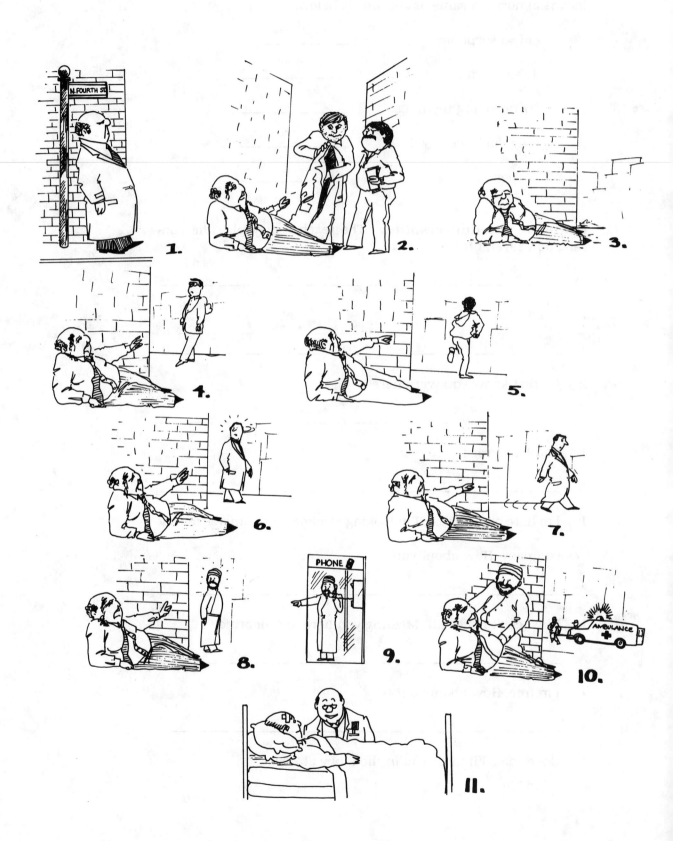

LISTENING COMPREHENSION

A. Discuss these questions with your class.

Did you ever need help when you ran out of gas, forgot your keys, hurt yourself? Who helped you? Tell the story to the class.

B. **Vocabulary** Talk about the new vocabulary words. If possible, point out the items in the story pictures. Repeat each word after the teacher.

mugged	*neighborhood*
beat	*acted*
alley	*dying*
passed	*church*

C. **First Listening** Look at the pictures and listen to the story as many times as you want. After you listen, tell the class any information you remember about the story.

D. **Listen and Choose** In this story, the speaker tells about the three men who saw him in the alley. Which man is the speaker talking about in each of these sentences? Listen again and write 1 for the first man, 2 for the second man, or 3 for the third man.

_____ 1. He went to the same church.

_____ 2. He dressed differently.

_____ 3. He called the police.

_____ 4. He said, "I'll be right back."

_____ 5. He felt sorry for me.

_____ 6. He acted like he didn't see me.

_____ 7. He was from my neighborhood.

153

_____ 8. He stayed with me.

E. **Listen and Number**   Listen to these sentences from the story. Write the number of the picture in the correct space.

1. _____   6. _____

2. _____   7. _____

3. _____   8. _____

4. _____   9. _____

5. _____   10. _____

F. **True or False**   Listen to these statements. Write T if the statement is true, F if the statement is false.

1. _____   6. _____

2. _____   7. _____

3. _____   8. _____

4. _____   9. _____

5. _____   10. _____

G. **Word Groups**   Listen to the story again. As you listen, write a few words which you can put in each group.

People   *Time*

    friend   *day*

_____   _____

_____   _____

_____   _____

_____   _____

H. Listen and STOP!   Read these sentences. Then listen to the tape again. When you hear a sentence that means almost the same as each sentence below, tell the teacher to stop the tape.

1. I was going to see a friend.
2. Some men attacked me.
3. A few minutes later, a man came by the alley.
4. He lived in the same area as I did.
5. He said that he was going to come back.
6. We were members of the same church.
7. It was almost night.
8. He was from a different country.
9. I thought he was going to leave me there.
10. Was he a neighbor of yours?

I.   With a Group   Talk about a time when you needed help or when you helped someone. Explain what happened.

LISTENING DISCRIMINATION

J.   Listen and Circle   You will hear two sentences. Decide if they are the same or different. Circle "same" or "different."

1. same	different	6. same	different
2. same	different	7. same	different
3. same	different	8. same	different
4. same	different	9. same	different
5. same	different	10. same	different

K.   **Listen and Write**   Listen to these sentences from the story. Write the verb you hear. All the verbs are in the regular past tense.

1. _____   6. _____

2. _____   7. _____

3. _____   8. _____

4. _____   9. _____

5. _____   10. _____

L.   **Listen and Write**   Listen to these sentences from the story. Write the verb you hear. All the verbs are in the irregular past tense.

1. _____   6. _____

2. _____   7. _____

3. _____   8. _____

4. _____   9. _____

5. _____   10. _____

M. **Fill In** Complete these sentences from the story with a verb in the past tense.

1. They _____ my coat and my money.

2. They _____ me in an alley to die.

3. A short time later, a man _____ by the alley.

4. I _____ , but he never _____ back.

5. I _____ I was dying and that I _____ help.

6. He _____ differently.

7. But he _____ me and _____ sorry for me.

8. He _____ the police.

9. He _____ with me and _____ for the ambulance.

10. "Who was he—a neighbor?" I _____ for a minute, then answered, "Yes, he _____ ."

N. **Prepositions** Complete these sentences with the correct preposition.

1. One day I was walking _____ North Fourth Street.

2. They left me _____ an alley to die.

3. He was _____ my neighborhood.

4. We went _____ the same church.

5. He wasn't _____ my country.

6. He saw me and felt sorry _____ me.

7. He stayed _____ me and waited _____ an ambulance.

CONVERSATION

O. Listen to the conversation a few times. Then, answer these questions.

Who is talking?
Where are they?
What injuries does the man have?
Who did the stranger call?
What does the man ask the stranger to do?
How can the man thank the stranger?

P. **Synonyms** Listen to the conversation again. Write a word that means almost the same as the words below.

injured   _____

okay   _____

Take it easy.   _____

arrives   _____

Q. **Complete the Conversation** The teacher may play the conversation several times.

Stranger: I just called the police. They'll be here in a minute. What

happened?

Man: _____

Stranger: You're hurt. You have a bad cut on your head. But you'll

be all right.

Man: _____

Stranger: Just relax. An ambulance is coming.

Man: _____

Stranger: Of course. Give me your number. I'll call after the

ambulance gets here.

Man: _____

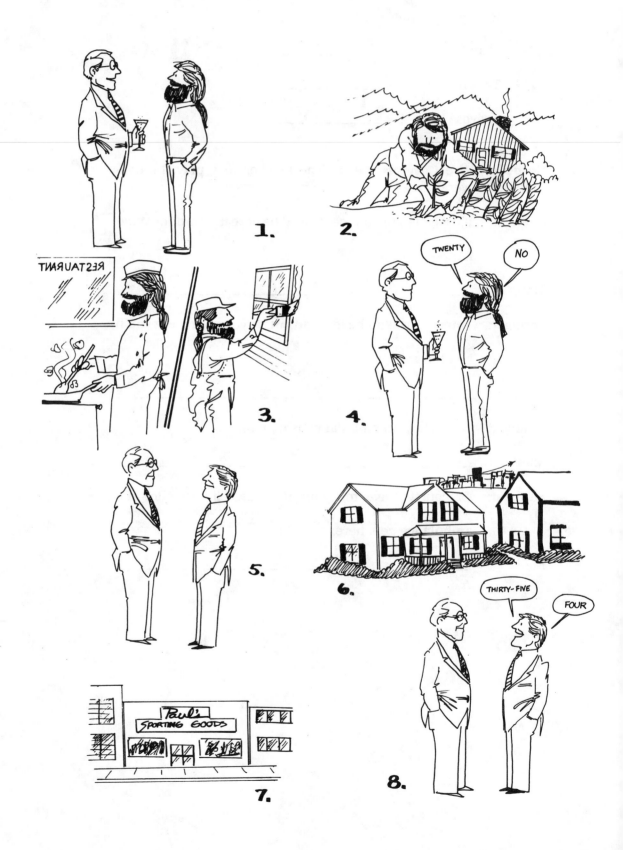

LISTENING COMPREHENSION

A. Discuss these questions with your class.

How old are you now? Think back five or ten years. Are the same things important to you now? What is one thing that is important to you now that wasn't important in the past?

B. **Vocabulary**   Talk about the new vocabulary words. If possible, point out the items in the story pictures. Repeat each word after the teacher.

cousin   waist
wore   on and on
beard   grew
living close to nature

C. **First Listening**   Look at the pictures and listen to the story as many times as you want. After you listen, tell the class any information you remember about the story.

D. **Listen and Choose**   As Paul got older, his ideas changed. Read these sentences. Which talk about Paul before? Which talk about him fifteen years later? Write B for before, L for later.

_____ 1. He lived in the mountains.

_____ 2. He spoke about the importance of the family.

_____ 3. He had a beard.

_____ 4. He grew his own food.

_____ 5. He had a small business.

_____ 6. He worked fifty hours a week.

_____ 7. He lived near the city.

_____ 8. He had no heat or electricity.

E. Listen and Number   Listen to these sentences from the story. Write the number of the picture in the correct space.

1. _____   6. _____

2. _____   7. _____

3. _____   8. _____

4. _____   9. _____

5. _____   10. _____

F. True or False   Listen to these statements. Write T if the statement is true, F if the statement is false.

1. _____   6. _____

2. _____   7. _____

3. _____   8. _____

4. _____   9. _____

5. _____   10. _____

G. Word Groups   Listen to the story again. As you listen, write a few words which you can put in each group.

Numbers

twice _____

_____

_____

_____

_____

Places

mountains _____

_____

_____

_____

_____

H. **Listen and STOP!** Read these sentences. Then listen to the tape again. When you hear a sentence that means almost the same as each sentence below, tell the teacher to stop the tape.

1. Paul is the son of my wife's uncle.
2. Paul liked to talk.
3. He lived in the country.
4. He had a large garden.
5. Paul liked living in the country, near nature.
6. I saw Paul again many years later.
7. He didn't have long hair or a beard.
8. He was still a happy person.
9. Paul worked long hours.
10. "Our lives change with the years."

I. **With a Group** Our ideas change as we get older. What is important to us is different when we are twenty from when we are forty. Make three lists. Write four things that are important to you now (present). Then think of three things that were important to you a few years ago (past) but are not as important now. Then, think of three things that will be important to you ten or twenty years from now (future). Discuss your lists with your group.

Present	*Past*	*Future*
_____	_____	_____
_____	_____	_____
_____	_____	_____
_____	_____	_____

LISTENING DISCRIMINATION

J.   Listen and Circle   You will hear two sentences. Decide if they are the same or different. Circle "same" or "different."

1. same   different   6. same   different

2. same   different   7. same   different

3. same   different   8. same   different

4. same   different   9. same   different

5. same   different   10. same   different

K.   Listen and Write   Listen to these sentences from the story. Write the verb you hear.

1. _____   6. _____

2. _____   7. _____

3. _____   8. _____

4. _____   9. _____

5. _____   10. _____

L. Fill In Complete these sentences from the story with a verb in the past tense.

1. I first _____ Paul at a family wedding.

2. He _____ a young man.

3. He _____ on and on about his life.

4. He _____ at different jobs for a few weeks.

5. I _____ Paul two questions.

6. This time he _____ a suit.

7. His hair _____ short and he _____ no beard.

8. He _____ in a house near the city.

9. He _____ about the importance of the family.

10. Then he_____ and said, "Times change."

M. Singular or Plural Listen to these sentences. Is the noun singular or plural? Circle the correct noun.

1. a. year, b. years

2. a. jean, b. jeans

3. a. house, b. houses, c. mountain, d. mountains

4. a. heat, b. heats

5. a. food, b. foods

6. a. money, b. monies, c. job, d. jobs

7. a. suit, b. suits

8. a. hair, b. hairs

9. a. store, b. stores

10. a. hour, b. hours, c. week, d. weeks

CONVERSATION

N.   Listen to the conversation a few times. Then, answer these questions.

Who's speaking?
Where are they?
Is this the first or second time that they are talking?
Where does Paul live?
What does he do for a living?

O. Synonyms Listen to the conversation again. Write a word that means almost the same as the words below.

I'm glad to meet you.   _____

walk in the mountains   _____

to make money   _____

for example   _____

make   _____

P. Complete the Conversation The teacher may play the conversation several times.

Paul: Hi. I'm Paul. I'm Judith's cousin.

Speaker: _____

           _____

Paul: Yes. I live in the mountains of Colorado.

Speaker: _____

Paul: Oh, I fish, hike, swim, play my guitar, work in my garden.

Speaker: _____

Paul: Small jobs, like I build tables or paint houses, you know.

Speaker: _____

Paul: It sure is. I'd never live in the city.

TAPESCRIPTS

1. Ali

My name is Ali. I'm from Egypt. I'm a student at Oakdale University. I live with my aunt and uncle. We live in a small apartment building. There are four families in this building.

There's a family of four living under us, the Ramirez family. They're from Mexico. Mr. Ramirez is a mailman. Mrs. Ramirez is a telephone operator. They have two boys—they're twins, Manuel and Mario. They're ten years old and in the fourth grade.

Next to us, there's a single man. He's from India. Mr. Pali is old; I think he's about 68 years old. He's a retired teacher. He has a lot of relatives, and they visit him a lot.

In the fourth apartment, there's a young couple from Vietnam, Cao and Ha Le. Cao's a student at Oakdale University. We're in the same English class and we walk to school together. Ha is an x-ray technician.

All the people in my apartment building are friendly. They're good neighbors.

E. Listen and Number   Look at the pictures and answer these questions with the correct number.
1. How many people live in Ali's apartment?
2. How many families live in this apartment building?
3. How many children do Mr. and Mrs. Ramirez have?
4. How old are the boys?
5. What grade are they in?
6. How many people live in the apartment next to Ali?
7. How old is Mr. Pali?
8. How many people live in this apartment building?

F. True or False   Listen to these statements. Write T if the statement is true, F if the statement is false.
1. Ali lives with his friends.
2. Ali lives in a two-family apartment building.
3. Ali lives next to Mr. and Mrs. Ramirez.
4. Mr. and Mrs. Ramirez both work.
5. Mario and Manuel are the same age.
6. Mr. Pali is retired.
7. Mr. Pali lives with his relatives.
8. Cao and Ali are friends.
9. Cao's wife is an x-ray technician.
10. The people in this building like one another.

J. Listen and Circle   Listen to these sentences from the story. Circle the verb you hear.
1. My name is Ali.
2. I'm from Egypt.
3. They're from Mexico.
4. Mrs. Ramirez is a telephone operator.
5. He's from India.
6. Cao is a student at Oakdale.
7. We're in the same English class.

8. Ha is an x-ray technician.
9. All the people in my apartment building are friendly.
10. They're good neighbors.

K. Listen and Write   Listen to these sentences from the story. Write the verb you hear.
1. I'm a student at Oakdale University.
2. There are four families in this building.
3. Mr. Ramirez is a mailman.
4. They're twins.
5. They're ten years old.
6. Mr. Pali is old.
7. He's a retired teacher.
8. Cao is a student at Oakdale.
9. All the people are friendly.
10. They're good neighbors.

L. There and They   Listen to these sentences from the story. Circle the first two words of each sentence.
1. There are four families in this building.
2. There's a family of four living under us.
3. They're from Mexico.
4. They're twins.
5. They're ten years old and in the fourth grade.
6. There's a single man in the apartment next to us.
7. There's a young couple from Vietnam in the fourth apartment.
8. They're good neighbors.

O. Conversation
Cao: Who is it?
Ali: It's me, Ali. Let's go!
Cao: Let's go?
Ali: Come on. We're late.
Cao: No, we're not. Remember, there's no English class today. The teacher has a meeting.
Ali: Oh! That's right! I forgot.
Cao: Come on in. Have a cup of coffee. The next class is an hour from now.
Ali: O.K. Sounds good.

2. Back in School

It's September 10th, the second week of school. This is the Dallas Adult School. There are classes for math, reading, and typing. And there are classes for English.

My class is in Room 201. I'm in Beginning English, the first class. This is my fourth year in the United States, but I don't speak

169

English. I only know a few words, like "girl" and "car" and "house."

I'm a little nervous about school. Maybe I'm too old to learn English. I'm 40 years old. English is difficult for me.

But, I want to learn English very much. This year my four children are in school. They all speak English. Sometimes, they speak English to each other, and I don't understand them. I want to talk to their friends and I want to talk to their teachers.

There are ten students in our class. Six are like me—they're from Mexico. Sonia, my sister, is in my class. My neighbor, Mr. Torres, is in my class, too. There are three students from Vietnam and one student from India.

Our teacher is Ms. Lang. She's young, only about 22 or 23. But she's a good teacher. I understand her. Her classes aren't too fast. She's patient with all of us.

Our class is three hours every day. It's from 9:00 to 12:00. There's a break at 10:30. We all go to the cafeteria and talk and drink coffee.

I enjoy school. It's not easy and we have a lot of homework. But I'm happy that I'm back in school.

E. Listen for Numbers   There are many numbers in this story. Answer each question with the correct number.
1. What's the date?
2. What is the room number?
3. How old is this woman?
4. How many children does she have?
5. How many students are in her class?
6. How many are from Mexico?
7. How many are from Vietnam?
8. How many are from India?
9. How old is the teacher?
10. How many hours is the class?
11. What time does the class begin?
12. What time is the break?

F. True or False   Listen to these statments. Write T if the statement is true, F if the statement is false.
1. This is the first day of school.
2. She knows a few words in English.
3. She is not nervous about school.
4. English is easy for her.
5. Her children speak English.
6. The class is small.
7. All of the students are from Mexico.
8. The teacher is a young man.
9. At the break, the students do their homework.
10. She is happy she is back in school.

J. Listen and Circle   Listen to these sentences from the story. Circle the verb you hear.
1. It's September 10th.
2. There are classes for English.
3. I'm in Beginning English.
4. English is difficult for me.
5. My four children are in school.
6. There are ten students in our class.
7. My neighbor is in my class.
8. Our teacher is Ms. Lang.
9. Our class is three hours.
10. I'm happy.

K. Listen and Write   Listen to these sentences from the story. Write the verb you hear.
1. There are classes for math and reading.
2. My class is in Room 201.
3. I'm a little nervous about school.
4. I'm 40 years old.
5. They're from Mexico.
6. There are three students from Vietnam.
7. She's a good teacher.
8. Her classes aren't too fast.
9. It's from 9:00 to 12:00.
10. There's a break at 10:30.

O. Conversation
Student: Hi Carmen. Where's your neighbor?
Carmen: Mr. Torres is sick today.
Student: What's the matter?
Carmen: He called me this morning. He has a bad cold.
Student: That's too bad. He's a good student.
Carmen: Yes. He's upset because he's not in school. But, Ms. Lang is giving me his papers.
Student: I hope he's better soon.

3. City or Country?

Gloria is a student in nursing school. She's going to graduate next month. She has two job offers. One is in a city hospital, the other is in a country hospital.

The hospital in the city is large; it's a 600-bed hospital. It's a cancer hospital. It gives excellent care to its patients. It's in a big city, near museums, theaters, and restaurants. The salary is high, $17,000 a year. But apartment rents are high, too.

The hospital in the country is small, it's a 50-bed hospital. It's a general hospital. It takes care of all kinds of patients. It's in a beautiful area, near lakes, rivers, and mountains. The salary is average—$14,000 a year. But apartment rents are low.

Gloria likes the city and the country. She doesn't know which hospital to choose.

E. Listen and Number   Listen to these sentences from the story. Write in the number of the correct picture.
1. It's in a big city.
2. The hospital in the country is small.
3. Apartment rents are low.
4. Gloria is a student in nursing school.
5. The salary is average.
6. It takes care of all kinds of patients.
7. It's near museums, theaters and restaurants.
8. Gloria has two job offers.
9. Apartment rents are high.
10. It's near lakes, rivers and mountains.

F. True or False   Listen to these statements. Write T if the statement is true, F if the statement is false.
1. Gloria is a student in nursing school.
2. She will finish school next month.

3. The hospital in the city has about 600 patients.
4. The hospital in the city is a general hospital.
5. The salary in the city hospital is low.
6. The hospital in the country takes care of all kinds of patients.
7. The hospital in the country is near theaters and museums.
8. Apartment rents are high in the city.
9. Apartment rents are high in the country, too.
10. Gloria likes the city more than the country.

J. Listen and Circle Listen to these sentences from the story. Circle the verb you hear.
1. Gloria is a student in nursing school.
2. One hospital is in the country.
3. The hospital in the city is large.
4. It's a 600-bed hospital.
5. It's a cancer hospital.
6. Apartment rents are high.
7. It's a general hospital.
8. It's in a beautiful area.
9. The salary is average.
10. Apartment rents are low.

K. Listen and Write Listen to these sentences from the story. Write the verb you hear, "is" or "are."
1. Gloria is a student in nursing school.
2. The other is in a country hospital.
3. It's a cancer hospital.
4. It's near museums, theaters, and restaurants.
5. The salary is high.
6. Apartment rents are high, too.
7. The hospital in the country is small.
8. It's a general hospital.
9. The salary is average.
10. Apartment rents are low.

L. Singular or Plural Listen to these sentences. Do you hear a singular or plural noun? Circle the word you hear.
1. Gloria has two job offers.
2. The hospital in the city is large.
3. It gives excellent care to its patients.
4. It's in a big city, near museums.
5. Apartment rents are high, too.
6. It's a 50-bed hospital.
7. It takes care of all kinds of patients.
8. It's in a beautiful area, near lakes.
9. The salary is average.
10. She doesn't know which hospital to choose.

O. Conversation

Gloria: Oh, Mom, what am I going to do?
Mother: Well, you know, we'd like you near us.
Gloria: I know.
Mother: And the country is so far from here.
Gloria: It is.
Mother: And you'd need a car in the country.
Gloria: That's right.
Mother: And all your friends are here.
Gloria: Hmmmm.
Mother: And what about David?
Gloria: Okay. That's it. I'm staying in the city.

4. The Job Interview

Mr. Johnson is the boss of Acme Trucking. His office is a mess. There are papers, books, and boxes everywhere. Nothing is clean, nothing is in order. He needs a good secretary.

Mrs. Santana wants the job. She's in his office for an interview. He's surprised because she's an older woman and she has no office experience.

Mrs. Santana is talking. "I'm the right person for this job. I'm a good typist. I took a typing course last year. I can type fifty words a minute. I'm a good talker and I'm friendly on the telephone. And I'm organized. You see, I'm a mother. I'm the mother of five children. At home, everything is organized. My house is clean and in order. I'm sure you want your office the same way."

Mr. Johnson is interested.

"Mr. Johnson, look at your office. Papers are everywhere. Your basket is full. The date on your calendar is the fifth. Today is the tenth. I can take care of everything in your office. And I'm a hard worker. Mr. Johnson, I'm the right person for this job."

Mr. Johnson is sitting in his chair and smiling. "Mrs. Santana, when can you start?"

E. Listen and Number Listen to these sentences from the story. Write in the number of the correct picture.
1. I can type fifty words a minute.
2. I'm the mother of five children.
3. Your basket is full.
4. His office is a mess.
5. I'm friendly on the phone.
6. The date on your calendar is the fifth.
7. Mrs. Santana is in his office for an interview.
8. There are papers, books and boxes everywhere.
9. Mr. Johnson is asking Mrs. Santana, "When can you start?"
10. My house is clean and in order.

F. True or False Listen to these statements. Write T if the statement is true, F if the statement is false.
1. Mrs. Santana is the boss of the company.
2. Mr. Johnson's office is clean and neat.
3. Mr. Johnson needs a good secretary.
4. Mrs. Santana has a lot of office experience.
5. Mrs. Santana can type well.
6. Mrs. Santana is an organized person.
7. Her house is a mess.
8. The date on Mr. Johnson's calendar is wrong.
9. Mrs. Santana is a hard worker.
10. Mrs. Santana is going to be Mr. Johnson's secretary.

K. Listen and Circle Listen to these sentences from the story. Circle the verb you hear.
1. Mr. Johnson is the boss of Acme Trucking.
2. His office is a mess.
3. There are papers, books, and boxes everywhere.
4. I'm the right person for this job.
5. I'm a good talker.
6. At home, everything is organized.
7. Mr. Johnson is interested.
8. Your basket is full.
9. The date on your calendar is the fifth.
10. I'm a hard worker.

L. Listen and Write   Listen to these sentences from the story. Write the verb you hear.
1. Nothing is clean.
2. She's in his office for an interview.
3. He's surprised.
4. I'm a good typist.
5. I'm friendly on the telephone.
6. I'm organized.
7. Mr. Johnson is interested.
8. Papers are everywhere.
9. Today is the tenth.
10. I'm the right person for this job.

N. Singular or Plural   Listen to these sentences. Do you hear a singular or plural noun? Circle the word you hear.
1. There are papers, books, and boxes everywhere.
2. He needs a good secretary.
3. She's an older woman.
4. She has no office experience.
5. I'm a good typist.
6. I took a typing course last year.
7. I can type fifty words a minute.
8. I'm the mother of five children.
9. Papers are everywhere.
10. Your basket is full.

O. Conversation

Mrs. Santana:	I got it! I got the job!
Mr. Santana:	At Acme Trucking?
Mrs. Santana:	Yes. I start on Monday.
Mr. Santana:	Congratulations! Tell me about it.
Mrs. Santana:	Well, it's a small company. It's a moving company. They have ten trucks.
Mr. Santana:	And what's your job?
Mrs. Santana:	I answer the telephone, type orders, and organize the office.
Mr. Santana:	Let's celebrate and go out for dinner.

5. Blowing a Fuse

It's 7:00 Monday morning. Everyone is awake at the Bentons'. Mr. and Mrs. Benton are getting ready for work. Larry and Ann are getting ready for school.

Mr. Benton is in the kitchen. He's fixing coffee in the coffee maker. Ann is in the kitchen, too. She's putting a piece of bread into the toaster. They're both listening to the radio. Mrs. Benton is in the living room. She's ironing her blouse. Larry is in the bathroom. He's blow drying his hair.

Suddenly, everything is quiet. There is no music from the radio. The coffee maker isn't working, and the toaster and the blow dryer are out, too. Mrs. Benton is looking at the iron, which is getting cold. The family blew a fuse.

Mr. Benton is going down to the basement with his flashlight. He's changing the fuse. The electricity is on again and everything is working.

E. Listen and Number   Listen to these sentences from the story. Which picture is each one describing? Write in the number of the correct picture.
1. Mrs. Benton is in the living room.
2. There is no music from the radio.
3. Larry is blow drying his hair.
4. The coffee maker isn't working.
5. Mr. Benton is going down to the basement.
6. Mr. Benton is fixing coffee in the coffee maker.
7. Mrs. Benton is ironing her blouse.
8. Mrs. Benton is looking at the iron, which is getting cold.
9. Mr. Benton is changing the fuse.
10. Ann is putting a piece of bread into the toaster.

F. True or False   Listen to these statements. Write T if the statement is true, F is the statement is false.
1. The family is getting ready for the day.
2. Mr. Benton is making coffee.
3. Mrs. Benton is fixing breakfast for the family.
4. Ann is in the living room.
5. Larry is blow drying his hair.
6. This family is using too much electricity.
7. The coffee maker, toaster, and iron aren't working.
8. They blew a fuse.
9. Mr. Benton is fixing the flashlight.
10. Mr. Benton is changing the fuse.

J. Listen and Circle   Listen to these sentences from the story. Circle the verb you hear.
1. Everyone is up at the Bentons'.
2. Mr. and Mrs. Benton are getting ready for work.
3. The children are getting ready for school.
4. Mr. Benton is fixing coffee in the coffee maker.
5. Ann is putting a piece of bread into the toaster.
6. They're both listening to the radio.
7. Mrs. Benton is in the living room.
8. Larry is blow drying his hair.
9. Everything is quiet.
10. The toaster and the blow dryer are out.

K. Listen and Write   Listen to these sentences from the story. Write the verb you hear.
1. Larry and Ann are getting ready for school.
2. Mr. Benton is fixing coffee.
3. Ann is putting a piece of bread into the toaster.
4. They're both listening to the radio.
5. Mrs. Benton is ironing her blouse.
6. Larry is blow drying his hair.
7. The coffee maker isn't working.
8. Mrs. Benton is looking at the iron.
9. Mr. Benton is going down to the basement.
10. He's changing the fuse.

O. Conversation

Mr. Benton:	Hm, what's the matter with the radio?
Ann:	I don't know, but the toaster isn't working either.
Larry:	Dad! My hair dryer isn't working.
Mrs. Benton:	And the iron is getting cold.
Mr. Benton:	Relax, everyone. We blew a fuse. Where's the flashlight?
Ann:	It's in the closet. Here it is, dad.
Mr. Benton:	Thanks. I'll go down and change the fuse. We can't use so many appliances at the same time.

6. The Supermarket

Oh, no! Here comes Mrs. Gomez with her four children. Every Friday night, it's the same story. The supermarket manager is watching them from the service counter, his hand on his head.

Mrs. Gomez is smiling, pushing her cart up and down the aisles. Aida, the youngest, is sitting in the cart, screaming. Mrs. Gomez isn't listening. She's at the meat counter, picking out some chicken. Aida is crying louder and louder. She wants ice cream.

Marco is helping his mother. He's putting food in the cart when she isn't looking. He's adding cookies, potato chips, and doughnuts.

The produce manager is talking to Carmen. He's telling her she can't eat the bananas. He's taking a bunch of grapes from her, too.

One of the employees is walking toward the manager. She's angry; she's pulling a child after her. While he was running, Juan Gomez knocked over five bottles of soda. Another employee is mopping the floor.

Thank goodness, Mrs. Gomez is finished. She's walking out of the store, pushing her cart. Her children are following quietly behind her.

"Good-bye." Mrs. Gomez is smiling at the manager. "We'll see you next week."

E. Listen and Number
Listen to these sentences from the story. Write the number of the picture in the correct space.
1. Aida, the youngest, is sitting in the cart, screaming.
2. The produce manager is taking a bunch of grapes from Carmen.
3. Mrs. Gomez is picking out some chicken.
4. Marco is putting food in the cart.
5. Mrs. Gomez is walking out of the store.
6. An employee is mopping the floor.
7. One of the employees is walking toward the manager. She is angry; she's pulling a child after her.
8. The supermarket manager is watching them from the service counter.
9. Here comes Mrs. Gomez with her four children.
10. Mrs. Gomez is smiling at the manager. "We'll see you next week."

F. True or False
Listen to these statements. Write T if the statement is true, F if the statement is false.
1. Mrs. Gomez shops at the same store every Friday night.
2. Mrs. Gomez is buying food for the week.
3. The youngest child is in the cart.
4. Mrs. Gomez has three children.
5. The children are staying with their mother in the supermarket.
6. Mrs. Gomez is watching her children carefully.
7. Marco is putting food in the basket.
8. Juan is pushing the cart for his mother.
9. Mrs. Gomez is angry with Juan.
10. The manager is happy when Mrs. Gomez is leaving the store.

J. Listen and Circle
You will hear two sentences. Decide if they are the same or different. Circle S or D. Listen for "is."
1. The supermarket manager is watching them.
   The supermarket manager watching them.
2. Mrs. Gomez is smiling.
   Mrs. Gomez is smiling.
3. Aida is crying louder and louder.
   Aida crying louder and louder.
4. Marco is helping his mother.
   Marco helping his mother.
5. The produce manager is talking to Carmen.
   The produce manager is talking to Carmen.
6. He's taking a bunch of grapes from her.
   He taking a bunch of grapes from her.
7. One of the employees is walking toward the manager.
   One of the employees is walking toward the manager.
8. She's pulling a child after her.
   She's pulling a child after her.
9. She's walking out of the store.
   She walking out of the store.
10. Mrs. Gomez is smiling.
    Mrs. Gomez is smiling.

K. Listen and Write
Listen to these sentences from the story. Write the verb you hear. Two of the verbs are negative.
1. Aida is sitting in the cart.
2. Mrs. Gomez isn't listening.
3. Aida is crying louder and louder.
4. Marco is helping his mother.
5. She isn't looking at him.
6. He's adding cookies, potato chips, and doughnuts.
7. One of the employees is walking toward the manager.
8. Another employee is mopping the floor.
9. She's walking out of the store, pushing her cart.
10. Her children are following quietly behind her.

M. Singular or Plural
Listen to these sentences. Is the noun singular or plural? Circle the correct noun.
1. Here comes Mrs. Gomez with her four children.
2. Every Friday night, it's the same story.
3. Mrs. Gomez is pushing her cart up and down the aisles.
4. She's picking out some chicken.
5. Marco is putting food in the cart.
6. He's adding cookies.
7. She can't eat the bananas.
8. He's taking a bunch of grapes from her.
9. One of the employees is walking toward the manager.
10. He knocked over five bottles of soda.

O. Conversation
Manager: Oh, no! Here's Mrs. Gomez again.
Employee: Mrs. Gomez?
Manager: You watch the TV monitor. I won't look. I'll tell you what's happening.
Employee: Okay.
Manager: The baby is screaming in the cart.
Employee: You can hear that.
Manager: Now, her little boy is filling the cart with cookies.
Employee: You're right. He is.
Manager: And the little girl is eating the fruit in the produce department.
Employee: Right again.
Manager: And the oldest boy is running around the store.
Employee: Yeah. And he just knocked over some soda. How did you know all that?
Manager: It's the same story every Friday night.

7. The Disco

Tonight I'm going to have a good time, Olga is saying to herself. Last Saturday was wonderful. I'm going to dance with him again.

Olga is standing at the bar with her friend Sonia. Many people are at the bar, eating and talking. Olga isn't watching them. She's looking at the dance floor. She knows lots of the people, but she's looking for someone special.

The band is playing a loud song. Almost everyone is dancing. Then, she sees him. He's dancing with someone else. Who is she? Is she his girlfriend? Well, there's no reason to stay. She's going home.

The music is stopping. His partner is walking away! He's staring at Olga. The band is beginning the next song and he's walking toward her. He's asking her to dance. As they walk onto the dance floor, Olga is smiling and so is he.

E. Listen and Number
Listen to these sentences from the story. Write the number of the correct picture next to each letter.
1. The band is playing a loud song.
2. His partner is walking away!
3. He's dancing with someone else.
4. They walk onto the dance floor.
5. Olga is standing at the bar.
6. He's walking toward her.
7. Olga is looking for someone special.
8. Olga is smiling.
9. He's staring at Olga.

F. True or False
Listen to these statements. Write T if the statement is true, F if the statement is false.
1. This is Olga's first time at the disco.
2. Olga can dance.
3. Olga is at the disco with her boyfriend.
4. Olga is looking for someone special.
5. Olga is eating at the bar.
6. Olga is dancing to a loud song.
7. He's dancing with someone else.
8. His partner is walking away.
9. Olga is asking him to dance.
10. Olga is happy because they are together again.

J. Listen and Circle
Listen to these sentences from the story. Circle the verb you hear.
1. Olga and her friend are standing at the bar.
2. Many people are at the bar.
3. Olga isn't watching them.
4. Olga is looking at the dance floor.
5. Almost everyone is dancing.
6. The band is playing a loud song.
7. Olga is going home.
8. The music is stopping.
9. His partner is walking away.
10. They're smiling.

K. Listen and Write
Listen to these sentences from the story. Write the verb you hear.
1. Many people are eating.
2. Many people are talking.
3. She's looking for someone special.
4. He's dancing.

5. Who is she?
6. His partner is walking away!
7. He's staring at Olga.
8. The band is beginning the next song.
9. He's asking her to dance.
10. Olga is smiling.

O. Conversation
Sonia: Do you see him? Is he here?
Olga: No, maybe he isn't here tonight.
Sonia: Look! Over there. Is that him in the blue shirt?
Olga: Sonia! Yes. And he's with another girl.
Sonia: Who is she?
Olga: I don't know. I don't care. I'm going home.
Sonia: Wait. The song's ending. She's walking away.
Olga: He's looking over here.
Sonia: Here he comes. Have a good time, Olga.

8. The Strike

It's cold, only 15°. It's February. It isn't snowing yet, but the sky is gray and heavy.

The workers are cold. None of them is inside the factory. They're outside, on strike. The workers are wearing heavy coats and hats and gloves. Several of them are standing around a garbage can. There's a fire inside. They're holding their hands over the fire and talking. One worker is handing out coffee. Other workers are walking up and down, trying to keep warm. They're carrying signs, "On Strike" and "10%" and "We Need More Sick Days."

Inside, it's hot, over 75°. The heat is on. Six people are sitting around the table. Their jackets are off, and they're sweating. The union leaders are sitting on one side, and the company bosses are on the other. Everyone is talking and shouting. The union has two demands. It's asking for a 10% increase in pay. The company is offering only 3%. The union is also asking for more sick days. Now, the workers have only three sick days. The union is asking for seven.

Today is the fifth day of the strike. Each side is tired and nervous. Everyone hopes there will be an agreement in two or three days.

E. Listen and Number
Look at the pictures and listen to the tape. Answer these questions with the correct number. Your answer can be "none."
1. What's the temperature outside?
2. How many people are standing around the garbage can?
3. How many workers are carrying signs?
4. How many workers are inside the factory?
5. How many workers are handing out coffee?
6. What's the temperature inside?
7. How many people are sitting at the table?
8. How many sick days do the workers have now?
9. What pay increase are the workers asking for?
10. How many days have the workers been on strike?

F. **True or False**   Listen to these statements. Write T if the statement is true, F if the statement is false.
1. It might snow.
2. The workers are inside the factory.
3. The workers are trying to keep warm.
4. There's a fire inside the garbage can.
5. The workers are sweating.
6. All of the workers are carrying signs.
7. The workers want more sick days.
8. The union leaders and the bosses are shouting.
9. The company is offering a 10% increase in pay.
10. Everyone is nervous about the strike.

J. **Listen and Circle**   Listen to these sentences from the story. Circle the verb you hear. Listen carefully for singular and plural.
1. It's cold.
2. It isn't snowing yet.
3. The workers are wearing heavy coats and hats and gloves.
4. Several of them are standing around a garbage can.
5. One worker is handing out coffee.
6. They're carrying signs.
7. The union leaders are sitting on one side.
8. Everyone is talking.
9. It's asking for a 10% increase in pay.
10. The company is offering only 3%.

K. **Listen and Write**   Listen to these sentences from the story. Write the verb you hear.
1. The sky is gray and heavy.
2. They're outside.
3. Several of them are standing around a garbage can.
4. They're holding their hands over the fire.
5. They're trying to keep warm.
6. They're carrying signs.
7. The union leaders are sitting on one side.
8. Everyone is shouting.
9. The union is asking for more sick days.
10. Each side is tired and nervous.

O. Conversation
Worker 1: I just got here. What's happening?
Worker 2: Not much. They're all inside. They're not telling us anything.
Worker 1: Five days already. When's it going to end?
Worker 2: Soon, I hope. It's freezing!
Worker 1: Yeah. Where's the coffee?
Worker 2: Over there. And get a sign, too.
Worker 1: Can I get you a cup of coffee, too?
Worker 2: Yes, thanks.

9. Retirement

Juan is a custodian in the Los Altos School System. He's mopping the front hall of his school, Los Altos Elementary School. It's an old building, but it's clean. It's always clean. Juan is a good worker.

Forty years. Forty years of mopping, cleaning, fixing. And after forty years, it's Juan's last day of work. He's sixty-five years old and it's time to retire.

Juan's mopping, but he isn't thinking about his work. What's he going to do with all his time? Yes, he and Luisa have plans. First, he's going to paint the house. Then, he's going to add a patio to the back of the house. His sons are going to help him. And at Christmas, they're going to fly to Florida to visit their daughter. But, best of all, he's going to fish. Juan is smiling now. No more Saturdays and Sundays with all the people and the noise. He's going to fish during the week. He's going to sit in his boat in peace and quiet. Well, maybe he is going to enjoy retirement.

Juan is putting his mop away. Charlie, Jose, Pete, and the others are coming through the front door. "Hey, come on Juan. You lucky guy. Your last day! We're taking you to B.J.'s Bar, then out to dinner. Let's go!"

E. **Listen and Number**   Listen to these sentences from the story. Write the number of the correct picture next to each letter.
1. Juan is going to fish during the week.
2. Juan is putting his mop away.
3. He's going to add a patio to the back of his house.
4. They're going to fly to Florida to visit their daughter.
5. Juan is going to paint the house.
6. He's going to sit in his boat in peace and quiet.
7. Juan is mopping the front hall of the school.
8. His friends are taking him out.
9. Juan isn't thinking about his work.
10. His sons are going to help him.

F. **True or False**   Listen to these statements. Write T if the statement is true, F if the statement is false.
1. Juan is forty years old.
2. It's his last day of work.
3. Juan works in a clean, new building.
4. Juan is thinking about his work.
5. Juan and his wife are going to move to Florida.
6. Juan is going to add a patio to the back of his house.
7. Juan likes to fish.
8. He's going to fish on the weekends.
9. It's the end of the workday.
10. Juan's friends from work are taking him out.

J. **Listen and Circle**   Listen to these sentences from the story. Some are in the present continuous tense; others are in the future. Circle the verb you hear.
1. Juan is mopping the front hall of his school.
2. What's he going to do with all his time?
3. He's going to paint the house.
4. He isn't thinking about his work.
5. He's going to add a patio to the back of the house.
6. They're going to fly to Florida.
7. Juan is smiling.
8. He's going to fish during the week.
9. Maybe he is going to enjoy retirement.
10. His friends are coming through the front door.

K. **Listen and Write**   Listen to these sentences from the story. Some of the verbs are in the present continuous tense; some are in the future. Write the verb you hear.
1. Juan is mopping the front hall.
2. What's he going to do with all his time?

3. He's going to add a patio to the back of the house.
4. His sons are going to help him.
5. They're going to visit their daughter.
6. He's going to fish.
7. He's going to sit in his boat in peace and quiet.
8. Juan is putting his mop away.
9. We're taking you to B.J.'s Bar.

O. Conversation

Charlie: How does it feel, Juan? Your last day of work!
Juan: Great! Tomorrow I'm going to sit in my boat and catch fish.
Pete: Be careful. You're going to get fat.
Juan: Don't worry. Luisa has lots of ideas for me around the house.
Charlie: Did you meet the new man yet?
Pete: Man? He's just a boy.
Juan: Yeah. I showed him around. You guys be nice to him.
Charlie: Are you going to come back and see us?
Juan: Of course. I'm going to miss you guys.

10. Eduardo

Eduardo is looking at his airline ticket again and smiling. Tomorrow he's going to be with his family in Cartagena. He's going to leave the snow and cold of New Jersey for the hot sun of his native Colombia.

Eduardo left Colombia almost three years ago. Are his family and friends going to think he's different? Are they going to understand his new life? He's bringing lots of pictures of America. He's going to show them his city, his car, and his apartment. But, he's also going to tell them about the long hours he works and how lonesome he feels.

Eduardo is packing his suitcase. He's looking at a picture of Yolanda. They went to the same high school together in Colombia and their parents are good friends. They've been writing for two years. At first, they wrote as friends. But now, their letters are more serious. They have plans for this vacation. They're going to go to the carnival together, attend a friend's wedding, and visit with Yolanda's family. How is he going to feel about her? How is she going to feel about him? Eduardo is going to return to America in one month. He's thinking, "Am I going to return alone? Or, am I going to have a wife at my side?"

E. Listen and Number
Listen to these sentences from the story. Write the number of the correct picture next to each letter.

1. Eduardo is packing his suitcase.
2. Eduardo is going to show his family pictures of America.
3. Now, their letters are more serious.
4. They're going to attend a friend's wedding.
5. Eduardo is looking at his airline ticket.
6. He's going to tell them about the long hours he works.
7. He's going to leave the snow and cold of New Jersey.

8. Eduardo is looking at a picture of Yolanda.
9. They're going to visit with Yolanda's family.
10. At first, they wrote as friends.

F. True or False
Listen to these statements. Write T if the statement is true, F if the statement is false.

1. Eduardo is going to leave for Colombia next month.
2. It's winter in New Jersey.
3. Eduardo is thinking about his vacation.
4. He's going to tell his family only the good things about America.
5. Eduardo has an easy life in America.
6. Eduardo knows Yolanda's parents.
7. Eduardo and Yolanda are going to see each other a lot this month.
8. They're going to attend a friend's wedding.
9. Eduardo is sure he wants to marry Yolanda.
10. Eduardo is going to stay in Colombia.

J. Listen and Circle
Listen to these sentences from the story. Circle the verb you hear.

1. Tomorrow, Eduardo is going to be with his family in Cartagena.
2. He's going to leave the snow and cold of New Jersey.
3. Are his family and friends going to think he's different?
4. Are they going to understand his new life?
5. He's going to show them pictures of his city.
6. He's going to tell them about the long hours he works.
7. They're going to go to the carnival.
8. They're going to visit with Yolanda's family.
9. Eduardo is going to return to America in one month.
10. Am I going to return alone?

K. Listen and Write
Listen to these sentences from and about the story. Write the verb you hear.

1. Tomorrow he's going to be with his family in Cartagena.
2. He's going to leave the snow and cold of New Jersey.
3. Are his family and friends going to understand his new life?
4. He's going to show them pictures of his apartment and his car.
5. Yolanda and Eduardo are going to attend a friend's wedding.
6. They're going to visit with Yolanda's family.
7. How are they going to feel about each other?
8. Am I going to have a wife at my side?
9. Is he going to ask her to marry him?
10. Eduardo is going to return to America in one month.

M. Listen and Write
Listen to these questions about the story. Answer with one of the following:

Yes, he is.   Yes, they are.
No, he isn't.   No, they aren't.

1. Is Eduardo going to leave tomorrow?
2. Is Eduardo going to live in Colombia?
3. Are his family and friends going to look at his pictures?
4. Is he going to tell them about his job?
5. Is Eduardo going to visit Yolanda's family?
6. Are Eduardo and Yolanda going to stay in Colombia?
7. Is Eduardo going to look for a job in Colombia?
8. Are Eduardo and Yolanda going to talk about their future?

O. Conversation

Passenger: Would you mind if I smoke?
Eduardo: No, go ahead.
Passenger: You're Colombian, aren't you?
Eduardo: Yes. How about you?
Passenger: Yes. I can't wait to get back home. I just spent the summer in New York.
Eduardo: I feel the same. I haven't seen my family in three years.
Passenger: Three years! That's a long time! Are you going to stay in Colombia now?
Eduardo: I'm only going to be here for a month.
Passenger: I like the United States, but Colombia is home.

11. Young Love

I'm Robert, Robert Charles. I'm a senior in high school. My girlfriend's name is Angela. Angela is beautiful. We have a wonderful time together. Tomorrow is her birthday. I'm going to take her out to a special restaurant. I have a surprise for her, an engagement ring. I'm going to ask her to marry me a few months after we graduate. At first, we're going to live in an apartment. Angela is a good typist, and she can work in an office for a year or two and we can save money for a house. I love children. Angela and I are going to have four or five. I already have a job. My father has a shoe store, and I'm going to continue the family business. I know that Angela is going to say "yes" when I give her the engagement ring. I understand her very well.

I'm Angela Hean. I'm a senior in high school. My boyfriend's name is Robert. Robert is handsome and kind. He's fun to be with. Tomorrow night, we're going to go out. I have a surprise for him. I have a scholarship to college. I'm going to go to college in the fall. I'm a good student, especially in science. I'm going to be a laboratory technician. I'm going to get married and have a small family someday, but I want a career, too. I like Robert very much, maybe I love him, but I want to be sure. I'm going to go out with other boys at school. I know Robert is going to be happy when I tell him about my scholarship. I understand him very well.

E. Listen and Number
Listen to these sentences from the story. Write the number of the correct picture next to each letter.

1. I'm going to go to college in the fall.
2. I'm going to continue the family business.
3. Angela can work in an office for a year or two.
4. I have a surprise for her, an engagement ring.
5. I'm going to go out with other boys at school.
6. Angela and I are going to have four or five children.
7. I'm going to be a laboratory technician.
8. I have a surprise for him. I have a scholarship to college.
9. I know that Angela is going to say "yes" when I give her the engagement ring.
10. I know that Robert is going to be happy when I tell him about my scholarship.

F. True or False
Listen to these statements. Write T if the statement is true, F if the statement is false.

1. Robert and Angela are in college.
2. Robert and Angela are going to get married in the fall.
3. Angela wants to be a secretary.
4. Robert is going to continue the family business.
5. Robert wants four or five children.
6. Angela wants four or five children.
7. Angela is going to be a laboratory technician.
8. Angela is going to go out with other boys.
9. Robert understands Angela.
10. Robert is going to be happy about Angela's scholarship.

J. Listen and Circle
Listen to these sentences from the story. Circle the verb you hear.

1. I'm Robert.
2. I'm a senior in high school.
3. Angela is beautiful.
4. Tomorrow is her birthday.
5. Angela is a good typist.
6. I'm going to take her out to a special restaurant.
7. We're going to live in an apartment.
8. Angela and I are going to have four or five children.
9. Angela is going to say "yes."
10. I'm going to go to college in the fall.

K. Listen and Write
Listen to these sentences from the story. Write the verb you hear.

1. I'm a senior in high school.
2. My boyfriend's name is Robert.
3. Robert is handsome and kind.
4. I'm going to ask her to marry me.
5. We're going to live in an apartment.
6. I'm going to continue the family business.
7. We're going to take her out.
8. I'm going to be a laboratory technician.
9. I'm going to have a small family.
10. Robert is going to be happy about my scholarship.

M. Articles
Listen to these sentences from the story. Some have the article "a"; others do not. If you hear "a," write it on the line. If not, put an "x."

1. I'm a senior in high school.
2. Angela is beautiful.
3. I have a surprise for her.
4. We can save money for a house.
5. I love children.
6. I already have a job.
7. Robert is kind.
8. He's fun to be with.
9. I'm going to have a small family someday.
10. I know Robert is going to be happy.

O. Conversation

Robert: Dad, I'm going to ask Angie to marry me.
Father: What are you going to do?
Robert: Ask Angie to marry me.
Father: Robert, you're too young. You're only eighteen.
Robert: I love her.
Father: How can you live on your salary from the store?
Robert: Angela is going to get a job, too.
Father: What about college?
Robert: I'm not going to college.

12. Divorce

Marsha and Ed Gibson are sitting at the kitchen table. Ed is nervous and upset, and he's smoking. Marsha's eyes are red. She looks tired. Their children, two boys eight and ten, are sitting with them. Tony and George know that their parents are having problems. They argue all the time. They don't talk to each other anymore. Their mom and dad aren't happy together anymore. Now, their parents are telling the boys that they're going to get a divorce.

Their mother is talking first. She's telling them that she loves them and their father loves them, too. But, she and their father are having problems. They aren't going to live together as a family anymore. It has nothing to do with the boys. The boys are going to live with her. They're going to stay in the same house, go to the same school, and be with all their friends.

Now, their father is talking. He's going to leave the house this weekend. He's not going to move far away; he's going to be in the next town. Two weekends a month, the boys are going to stay with him. And, they're going to be with him one month in the summertime. He'll take his vacation then and they'll go to the beach. The boys can call him anytime. He's going to be near. It'll be better this way.

Tony and George don't really understand what's happening. They know that their parents aren't happy. But, they want everyone to stay together.

E. Listen and Number   Listen to these sentences from the story. Write the number of the picture in the correct space.
1. The boys can call their father anytime.
2. Ed and Marsha are going to get a divorce.
3. Two weekends a month, the boys are going to stay with him.
4. Ed is nervous and upset, and he's smoking.
5. They're going to stay in the same house.
6. Tony and George don't really understand what's happening.
7. They'll go to the beach in the summertime.
8. Ed is going to leave the house this weekend.
9. The boys are going to go to the same school.
10. He's not going to move far away.

F. True or False   Listen to these statements. Write T if the statement is true, F if the statement is false.
1. The family is in the kitchen.
2. Ed and Marsha are having problems with their children.
3. Ed and Marsha love their children very much.
4. The boys are going to live with their mother.
5. The boys are going to go to a new school.
6. Their father is going to move far away.
7. Ed wants to see his sons often.
8. The boys can call their father any day they want to.
9. Tony and George are upset about the divorce.
10. The boys understand why their parents are getting a divorce.

J. Listen and Circle   Listen to these sentences from the story. Circle the verb you hear.
1. Marsha and Ed Gibson are sitting at the kitchen table.
2. Ed's smoking.
3. Their parents are going to get a divorce.
4. They are having problems.
5. The boys are going to stay in the same house.
6. Their father is talking.
7. He's going to leave this weekend.
8. He's not going to move far away.
9. They're going to be with him one month in the summer.
10. He's going to be near.

K. Listen and Write   Listen to these sentences from the story. Write the verb you hear.
1. The children are sitting with them.
2. They're always arguing.
3. Ed and Marsha are going to get a divorce.
4. They aren't going to live together anymore.
5. The boys are going to live with her.
6. They're going to go to the same school.
7. Now, their father is talking.
8. He's going to leave the house this weekend.
9. He's going to be in the next town.
10. Two weekends a month, the boys are going to stay with him.

O. Conversation
Father: Come on, kids, in the car. Did you eat lunch yet?
Son: No, we're hungry.
Father: Let's go to McDonald's.
Son: OOh! Can I have a big Mac?
Father: Sure. Anything you want.
Son: What are we going to do this weekend?
Father: Would you like to go to a baseball game?
Son: Wow! Who's playing?
Father: The Yankees and the Angels. And I have three tickets for tomorrow's game.

13. Two Officers

Officer Pappas reports to the police station at 11 p.m. each evening. He works the night shift. His partner is Officer Frezza, a female officer.

Pappas and Frezza patrol the east side of town. There are many robberies at night. Pappas drives slowly up and down the streets. Frezza looks carefully at the stores and houses. She watches for strangers and open windows.

In their patrol car, Pappas and Frezza listen to the police radio. Family fights are common at night. Loud parties are another problem. When the two officers arrive, most people quiet down. At times, Pappas and Frezza make an arrest.

As they drive, the two officers watch for drunk drivers. When they see a car speeding, Pappas turns on the red flashing lights. He stops the driver. If the driver is drunk, they arrest him and bring him to the police station.

Most nights, Pappas and Frezza drive over 150 miles. They usually make two or three arrests and write several tickets. At 7:00 a.m., when most people wake up for work, Pappas and Frezza go home.

E. Listen and Number   Listen to these sentences from the story. Write the number of the picture in the correct space.

1. They listen to the police radio.
2. Pappas reports to the police station at 11 p.m. each night.
3. If the driver is drunk, they arrest him and bring him to the police station.
4. At 7:00 a.m., they leave for home.
5. Family fights and loud parties are common problems.
6. Pappas drives slowly up and down the street.
7. He turns on the flashing red lights.
8. When the officers arrive, most people quiet down.
9. Frezza looks carefully at the stores and houses.
10. His partner is Frezza, a female officer.

F. True or False   Listen to these statements. Write T if the statement is true, F if the statement is false.

1. Pappas works the day shift.
2. His partner is a woman.
3. Pappas and Frezza walk slowly up and down the streets.
4. Frezza watches for signs of a robbery.
5. The police radio tells the officers the location of family fights.
6. Pappas and Frezza always arrest people who are fighting.
7. The officers also watch for drunk drivers.
8. They always arrest drivers who are drunk.
9. The officers drive many miles each night.
10. Frezza sleeps during the day.

J. Listen and Circle   Listen to these sentences from the story. Circle the verb you hear.

1. Officer Pappas reports to the police station at 11 p.m.
2. He works the night shift.
3. Pappas and Frezza listen to the police radio.
4. Family fights are common at night.
5. At times, the officers make an arrest.
6. They watch for drunk drivers.
7. Pappas turns on the red flashing lights.
8. He stops the driver.
9. They arrest him.
10. They bring him to the police station.

K. Listen and Write   Listen to these sentences from the story. Write the verb you hear.

1. His partner is Officer Frezza.
2. Pappas and Frezza patrol the east side of town.
3. Pappas drives slowly up and down the streets.
4. Frezza watches for open windows.
5. Most people quiet down.
6. The officers drive over 150 miles a night.
7. They usually make two or three arrests.
8. They write several tickets.
9. Pappas goes home.
10. Pappas and Frezza go home.

M. Singular or Plural   Listen to these sentences. Do you hear a singular or plural noun? Circle the word you hear.

1. Pappas works the night shift.
2. His partner is Officer Frezza.

3. There are many robberies at night.
4. Frezza looks carefully at the stores and houses.
5. Family fights are common at night.
6. At times, Pappas and Frezza make an arrest.
7. They watch for drunk drivers.
8. He stops the driver.
9. Pappas and Frezza drive over 150 miles.
10. They write several tickets.

O. Conversation

Mr. White: Hello, officers.
Officer: We'd like to speak to the owner of this house.
Mr. White: I'm the owner, Mr. White.
Officer: Mr. White, we have several complaints from your neighbors. They're not too happy about the noise.
Mr. White: It's my daughter's graduation party. I didn't realize the music was so loud.
Officer: You can hear it a block away. It's 2:00 a.m.
Mr. White: I'm sorry. They'll quiet down.

14. Ana and Peter

Ana gets up at 5:15 a.m. four mornings a week. She showers, dresses, and eats breakfast. She leaves her husband and children, who are still sleeping, by 6:00 a.m. Ana is an airline pilot, and she flies the daily shuttle from New York to Boston. Her husband, Peter, is a househusband. He stays home with the children, ages two, six, and eight.

Peter likes staying home. He says that most fathers don't spend enough time with their children. He enjoys his family. It's a lot of work. In the morning, he cleans, shops, and does the laundry. In the afternoon, when the youngest takes a nap, he fixes TV sets. He has a small business at home. When the children come home from school, they take bike rides or play outside. Then, it's time for homework.

Ana is usually home by 6:00 p.m. After dinner, she plays with the children and reads to them. When they're in bed, Peter and Ana have some time to themselves.

But some days Ana doesn't get home until late. On those days, she doesn't see the children.

Tonight, it's eight o'clock and Ana is still in Boston. She's calling Peter. The weather is bad and the flight is going to be late. Peter is telling her not to worry. The children can see her tomorrow. Peter misses Ana when she isn't home at night. But, he also knows how much she likes her job. He'll stay up and wait for her.

E. Listen and Number   Listen to these sentences from the story. Write in the number of the correct picture.

1. Peter cleans the house.
2. They take bike rides.
3. Peter and Ana have some time to themselves.
4. Ana gets up at 5:15.
5. He fixes TV sets.
6. She reads to the children.

7. Ana is an airline pilot.
8. The weather is bad and the flight is going to be late.
9. He shops for the family.
10. Peter will stay up and wait for her.

F.   True or False   Listen to these statements. Write T if the statement is true, F if the statement is false.

1. Ana says goodbye to the children in the morning.
2. Ana works five days a week.
3. Peter does most of the housework.
4. Peter takes a nap in the afternoon.
5. Peter enjoys his children.
6. Ana is always home for dinner.
7. Ana is calling from New York.
8. Ana likes her job.
9. Peter and Ana have busy lives.
10. Peter wants Ana to stop working.

J.   Listen and Circle   Listen to these sentences from the story. Circle the verb you hear.

1. Ana gets up at 5:15 a.m.
2. She leaves her husband and children by 6:00 a.m.
3. Peter stays home with the children.
4. He enjoys his family.
5. After school, they take bike rides.
6. They play outside.
7. Ana reads to the children.
8. Peter and Ana have some time to themselves.
9. On those days, she doesn't see the children.
10. She likes her job.

K.   Listen and Circle   You will hear two sentences. Decide if they are the same or different. Circle "same" or "different."

1. She showers.
   She showers.
2. She flies the daily shuttle.
   She fly the daily shuttle.
3. He cleans the house.
   He clean the house.
4. The youngest takes a nap.
   The youngest take a nap.
5. They play outside.
   They play outside.
6. She play with the children.
   She plays with the children.
7. She reads to the children.
   She reads to the children.
8. Peter and Ana have some time for themselves.
   Peter and Ana have some time for themselves.
9. She doesn't see the children.
   She doesn't see the children.
10. She likes her job.
    She like her job.

L.   Listen and Write   Listen to these sentences from the story. Write the verb you hear.

1. Ana gets up at 5:15 a.m.
2. She eats breakfast.
3. He enjoys his family.
4. He does the laundry.
5. He has a small business at home.
6. They take bike rides.

7. After dinner, she reads to the children.
8. Some days Ana doesn't get home until late.
9. Peter misses Ana at night.
10. She likes her job.

O.   Conversation

Son: What time's Mom getting home tonight?
Father: She's going to be late.
Son: Can we stay up until she comes home?
Father: No. I don't know what time she's going to be home. Let's make some popcorn.
Son: Can I put it in the popcorn popper?
Father: You can get out the popcorn. I'll put it in the popcorn popper.
Son: Then can we play a game?
Father: Then, you can go to bed.

15. Good Health

Leonid just turned fifty last week. He's a successful businessman. He owns a large printing company. He lives in a beautiful home with his wife and two daughters. He drives an expensive car and wears the best clothes. He has everything that money can buy, except for one thing, good health.

It happened one evening as he was leaving the office. All day he felt a shortness of breath. He was a little dizzy. He remembers the terrible pains in his chest as he collapsed. For two weeks Leonid lay in the intensive care unit of the hospital. Before leaving the hospital, Leonid got his orders from the doctor. He's trying to follow them.

Leonid has to lose weight and exercise each day. He can't smoke or drink. Before work, Leonid has to walk one mile. He can't have his usual sausage and eggs breakfast. And he has to drink decaffeinated coffee. For lunch, he can't order the salty french fries that he loves so much. For dinner, he has to eat fish or chicken and a vegetable. Leonid hates vegetables and he dreams about steak.

Leonid also has to slow down at the office. At first, he can only work four hours a day. He can increase his hours each month, but he can never work more than seven hours a day. After work, he has to exercise at a local health club. Leonid misses the long hours and the excitement of the office. How did this happen to him? He's only fifty years old.

E.   Listen and Number   Listen to these sentences from the story. Write the number of the picture in the correct space.

1. Leonid can't smoke.
2. Leonid has to slow down at the office.
3. He drives an expensive car.
4. He remembers the terrible pains in his chest.
5. For dinner, he has to eat fish or chicken.
6. He has to walk one mile before breakfast.
7. Leonid got his orders from the doctor.

8. After work, he has to exercise at a local health club.
9. He lives in a beautiful home with his wife and two daughters.
10. He has to drink decaffeinated coffee.

F. True or False Listen to these statements. Write T if the statement is true, F if the statement is false.
1. Today is Leonid's birthday.
2. Leonid is a rich man.
3. Leonid broke his leg when he was leaving work.
4. Leonid had a small heart attack.
5. Leonid is tall and thin.
6. Leonid is following the doctor's orders.
7. Leonid has to exercise every day.
8. Leonid likes his new diet.
9. Leonid has to work seven hours a day.
10. Leonid likes his job.

J. Listen and Circle You will hear two sentences. Decide if they are the same or different. Circle "same" or "different."
1. Leonid owns a large printing company.
   Leonid own a large printing company.
2. He lives in a beautiful home.
   He lives in a beautiful home.
3. He drives an expensive car.
   He drive an expensive car.
4. He have everything that money can buy.
   He has everything that money can buy.
5. He wears the best clothes.
   He wears the best clothes.
6. It happened one evening.
   It happens one evening.
7. He remembers the pains in his chest.
   He remembers the pains in his chest.
8. Leonid has to lose weight.
   Leonid has to lose weight.
9. He hate vegetables.
   He hates vegetables.
10. He misses the long hours.
    He misses the long hours.

K. Listen and Write Listen to these sentences from the story. Write the verb you hear. All of the verbs are in the present tense.
1. He's a successful businessman.
2. He owns a large printing company.
3. He lives in a beautiful home.
4. He drives an expensive car.
5. He wears the best clothes.
6. He remembers the terrible pains in his chest.
7. He has to walk one mile before work.
8. He dreams about steak.
9. He has everything, except good health.
10. Leonid misses the excitement of the office.

L. Listen and Write Listen to these sentences from the story. Write the complete verb you hear. Listen for "has to," "can," or "can't."
1. He has to lose weight.
2. He can't smoke.
3. He can't drink.

4. He has to walk one mile before work.
5. He can't have his usual sausage and eggs breakfast.
6. He has to drink decaffeinated coffee.
7. He can't order the salty french fries that he loves.
8. He has to eat fish or chicken for dinner.
9. At first, he can only work four hours a day.
10. He can increase his hours each month.

M. Listen and Write Listen to these questions about the story. Answer with "Yes, he can." or "No, he can't."
1. Can Leonid smoke?
2. Can Leonid drink?
3. Can Leonid eat sausage and eggs for breakfast?
4. Can he drink decaffeinated coffee?
5. Can he drink regular coffee?
6. Can he eat fish?
7. Can he eat steak?
8. Can Leonid go to work?
9. Can he increase his hours each month?
10. Can he work eight hours a day?

O. Conversation

Doctor: You can put your shirt back on. Your heart sounds strong.

Leonid: I feel stronger, too. I don't get tired so easily.

Doctor: And you're down five more pounds.

Leonid: Maybe I am, but I hate this diet. Everything I like is no good for me.

Doctor: Stay with the diet.

Leonid: It's the coffee that I miss the most. A good cup of coffee in the morning.

Doctor: The caffeine is no good for you.

Leonid: How about work? I'm working five hours a day now. Can I add another hour?

Doctor: Yes. Try it and see how you feel. If you're tired, go back to five.

16. Friday the 13th

Hiro hears his alarm and turns on the radio. He hears the announcer say, "Good morning, everyone. And I hope it's a good day for you, not an unlucky one. It's Friday, the 13th. It's cold and rainy outside. It's a good day to stay home, if you can."

What's unlucky about Friday, the 13th? Hiro dresses and goes into the kitchen. He opens the refrigerator. Where's the orange juice? Hiro looks in the back of the refrigerator. He knocks a carton of milk off the shelf. The milk spills on his pants and shoes and covers the floor. He cleans up the mess and runs to change his clothes. By now, he's late for work. Where are his car keys? He looks everywhere, then finally opens the refrigerator again. There they are, on the top shelf. He can't find his umbrella, so he runs through the rain to his car. The seat is all wet because he didn't close the window last night. Hiro puts the key in the ignition and turns it. The engine starts, then dies. He tries again, but the same thing happens. Hiro looks at the gas gauge. It's on empty.

Hiro leaves his car and goes back in the house. He takes off his clothes and gets back into bed. It's Friday the 13th, a good day to stay home.

E. Listen and Number   Listen to these sentences from the story. Write the number of the picture in the correct space.
1. Where's the orange juice?
2. Hiro takes off his clothes and gets back in bed.
3. His keys are on the top shelf.
4. The gas gauge is on empty.
5. Hiro cleans up the mess.
6. Hiro hears his alarm and turns on the radio.
7. The seat is all wet.
8. Hiro knocks a carton of milk off the shelf.
9. The engine starts, then dies.
10. Hiro opens the refrigerator.

F. True or False   Listen to these statements. Write T if the statement is true, F if the statement is false.
1. It's a cold, rainy day.
2. It's a Monday morning.
3. It's a work day for Hiro.
4. Hiro spills the orange juice.
5. Hiro has to change his clothes.
6. Hiro can't find his car keys.
7. Hiro finds his car keys in his bedroom.
8. Hiro uses his umbrella when he runs to the car.
9. Hiro has no gas in his car.
10. Today is a lucky day for Hiro.

J. Listen and Circle   You will hear two sentences. Decide if they are the same or different. Circle "same" or "different."
1. Hiro hears his alarm.
   Hiro hear his alarm.
2. He turns on the radio.
   He turns on the radio.
3. Hiro dresses and go into the kitchen.
   Hiro dresses and goes into the kitchen.
4. Hiro looks in the back of the refrigerator.
   Hiro look in the back of the refrigerator.
5. He knocks a carton of milk off the shelf.
   He knocks a carton of milk off the shelf.
6. He looks everywhere.
   He looks everywhere.
7. He runs through the rain to his car.
   He runs through the rain to his car.
8. He puts the key in the ignition.
   He puts the key in the ignition.
9. The engine starts, then die.
   The engine starts, then dies.
10. He try again.
    He tries again.

K. Listen and Write   Listen to these sentences from the story. Write the verb you hear.
1. Hiro opens the refrigerator.
2. The milk spills on his pants.
3. It covers the floor.

4. He cleans up the mess.
5. He looks everywhere for his keys.
6. Hiro turns the key.
7. He looks at the gas gauge.
8. Hiro leaves his car.
9. He takes off his clothes.
10. He gets back into bed.

O. Conversation
John: American Engineering. John Trady speaking.
Hiro: John, this is Hiro.
John: Hiro! What's the problem? You're not at your desk.
Hiro: I don't feel well. I'm not coming in today.
John: What's the matter?
Hiro: I'm not sure. I have an upset stomach and a terrible headache.
John: Just take it easy. I'll tell the boss. Is there anything here you need me to do?
Hiro: No, everything on my desk can wait for Monday.
John: Okay. Take care.

17. Fast Thinking

Last month, the Wilsons went to Green Trees Park. Jim and Sally sat under the trees and talked and read. The children played ball.

Sally decided to take a picture of the children. She took her camera and walked over to them. She focused her camera. Then, she heard a scream. Sally looked up. A man was stealing a woman's purse. He was running in her direction.

Sally thought fast. She took three pictures of the man. When the police came, she gave them the film.

The next day, one of Sally's photographs was in the newspaper. Under it was the story of the robbery. In a few hours, the police knew the man's name and address. They went to his house and arrested him. The man is now serving three months in jail.

E. Listen and Number   Listen to these sentences from the story. Write the number of the picture in the correct space.
1. One of Sally's photographs was in the newspaper.
2. The Wilsons went to the park.
3. Sally took out her camera.
4. When the police came, Sally gave them the film.
5. She focused her camera.
6. Jim and Sally sat under the trees and talked and read.
7. A man was stealing a woman's purse.
8. Sally walked over to the children.
9. The man is now serving three months in jail.
10. The police arrested the man.

F. True or False   Listen to these statements. Write T if the statement is true, F if the statement is false.
1. Jim played ball with the children.
2. Jim and Sally sat under the trees.

3. Sally decided to take a picture of the children.
4. One of the children screamed.
5. A man was stealing a woman's purse.
6. The man took Sally's camera.
7. Sally didn't know what to do.
8. Sally gave her film to the police.
9. The three pictures were in the newspaper.
10. The police arrested the man the next day.

J. Listen and Circle
You will hear two sentences. Decide if they are the same or different. Circle "same" or "different."

1. The Wilsons went to the park.
   The Wilsons go to the park.
2. Jim and Sally sat under a tree.
   Jim and Sally sat under a tree.
3. Sally takes out her camera.
   Sally took out her camera.
4. She hears a scream.
   She heard a scream.
5. Sally thought fast.
   Sally thought fast.
6. She took three pictures.
   She takes three pictures.
7. The police come.
   The police came.
8. One of the photographs was in the newspaper.
   One of the photographs was in the newspaper.
9. The police knew his name and address.
   The police know his name and address.
10. They went to his house.
    They go to his house.

K. Listen and Write
You will hear a statement in the past tense. Write the verb you hear.

1. The Wilsons went to the park.
2. Jim and Sally sat under the trees.
3. Sally took her camera.
4. She heard a scream.
5. Sally thought fast.
6. She took three pictures of the man.
7. She gave the film to the police.
8. One of the photographs was in the newspaper.
9. In a few hours, the police knew the man's name.
10. They went to his house.

O. Conversation

Sally: Hello.
Policeman: Mrs. Wilson, Officer Brown.
Sally: Yes. Did you find the man?
Policeman: We arrested him today.
Sally: So soon?
Policeman: One of his neighbors called. She saw his picture in the newspaper.
Sally: Where is he now?
Policeman: In jail. He's going to be there for three months. We want to thank you for your help.
Sally: I just took a few pictures.
Policeman: And those pictures gave us the man we wanted. Thank you again.
Sally: It was nothing.

18. Two Brothers

Alan and Jack Stein are brothers. They don't see each other very often. Alan lives in Ohio. Jack lives in Texas.

Alan is on vacation in California. He is staying at the Sands Hotel in San Francisco. This morning, he visited an art museum. In the afternoon, he went sightseeing. He got back to the hotel at 6:00. He put on his bathing suit and went down to the pool. He swam for a few minutes, then sat down on a chair by the side of the pool and picked up a newspaper.

Alan doesn't know that his brother Jack is in California. Jack is staying at the Sands Hotel in San Francisco, too. Jack's company sent him to a conference there. This morning, he had two meetings. In the afternoon, there were more meetings. Jack got back to the hotel at 6:10. He put on his bathing suit and went down to the pool. He swam for a few minutes, then sat down on a chair by the side of the pool and picked up a newspaper.

A waitress came by and asked the two men, "Would you like something to drink?" They put down their newspapers at the same time and both said, "Yes, please, a martini," Then they looked at each other in surprise. "Alan!" "Jack!" "I can't believe it!"

E. Listen and Number
Listen to these sentences from the story. Write the number of the picture in the correct space.

1. This morning, he visited an art museum.
2. Jack is staying at the Sands Hotel in San Francisco.
3. In the afternoon, there were more meetings.
4. A waitress came by and asked the two men, "Would you like something to drink?"
5. Jack lives in Texas.
6. Alan swam for a few minutes.
7. Jack put on his bathing suit.
8. In the afternoon, he went sightseeing.
9. Jack sat down by the side of the pool and picked up a newspaper.
10. They looked at each other in surprise.

F. True or False
Listen to these statements. Write T if the statement is true, F if the statement is false.

1. Jack and Alan see each other a lot.
2. Alan and Jack are in California on business.
3. Alan and Jack are staying in the same room in the hotel.
4. Alan went sightseeing in the afternoon.
5. Alan swam in the pool for a few minutes.
6. Jack had several meetings.
7. Jack got back to the hotel a few minutes after Alan.
8. Jack sat down by the side of the pool.
9. Jack and Alan both ordered a beer.
10. Jack didn't know that Alan was in California.

J. Listen and Circle
Listen to these sentences from the story. Circle the verb you hear.

1. They don't see each other very often.
2. Jack lives in Texas.
3. He visited an art museum.
4. He got back to the hotel at 6:00.
5. He sat down on a chair by the side of the pool.
6. He is staying at the Sands Hotel in San Francisco.
7. This morning, he had two meetings.

8. The waitress asked the two men, "Would you like something to drink?"
9. They looked at each other in surprise.
10. I can't believe it!

K. Listen and Write Listen to these sentences from the story. Write the verb you hear. All the verbs are in the past tense.

1. This morning, he visited an art museum.
2. In the afternoon, he went sightseeing.
3. He got back to the hotel at 6:00.
4. He put on his bathing suit.
5. He swam for a few minutes.
6. He sat down by the side of the pool.
7. He picked up a newspaper.
8. His company sent him to a conference.
9. He had two meetings.
10. In the afternoon, there were more meetings.

O. Conversation

Alan: Jack!
Jack: Alan!
Alan: I can't believe it!
Jack: I didn't know you were here!
Alan: And I didn't know you were here!
Jack: You look great!
Alan: You do, too. Why are you here in California?
Jack: I'm here on business. I'm looking at some new cameras for my company. How about you?
Alan: I love San Francisco. I'm here for a few days on vacation.
Jack: I just can't believe it! Meeting you here in California!
Alan: What are you doing tonight?
Jack: I'm free. How about you?
Alan: The same. Let's go out for dinner.
Jack: Good idea. I'll meet you in the lobby at 7:00.

19. My Neighbor

One day I was walking down North Fourth Street. I was going to visit a friend. As I was walking past a park, several men jumped out and mugged me. They took my coat and my money. They beat me, then left me in an alley to die.

A short time later, a man passed by the alley. He was from my neighborhood. I shouted. I knew he was going to help me. He said, "I'll get some help." Then, he left. I waited, but he never came back.

A few hours later, a second man passed the alley. I called him. I knew he was going to help me because we went to the same church. But he acted like he didn't see me. He turned and left.

It was getting late. I knew I was dying and that I needed help. It was almost dark when a third man passed the alley. I didn't know him. He dressed differently. He wasn't from my country. I didn't think he was going to help me. But he saw me and felt sorry for me. He stopped and called the police. He stayed with me and waited for the ambulance.

The next day, the doctor said to me, "It's a good thing that man stopped and helped you. You almost died. Who was he—a neighbor?"

I thought for a minute, then answered, "Yes, he was."

E. Listen and Number Listen to these sentences from the story. Write the number of the picture in the correct space.

1. He stopped and called the police.
2. We went to the same church.
3. He dressed differently.
4. Several men jumped out and mugged me.
5. The next day, the doctor talked to me.
6. They left me in an alley to die.
7. One day I was walking down North Fourth Street.
8. He said, "I'll get some help."
9. He stayed with me and waited for the ambulance.
10. He acted like he didn't see me.

F. True or False Listen to these statements. Write T if the statement is true, F if the statement is false.

1. I was going to the store.
2. Some men mugged me.
3. They took my car and my money.
4. One of my neighbors passed the alley.
5. He said that he was going for help.
6. A man from my church passed the alley.
7. He stopped and helped me.
8. I was in the alley for many hours.
9. A policeman walked by and saw me in the alley.
10. The man who helped me dressed differently.

J. Listen and Circle You will hear two sentences. Decide if they are the same or different. Circle "same" or "different."

1. Several men jumped out.
   Several men jump out.
2. They mugged me.
   They mugged me.
3. I shout.
   I shouted.
4. He turned and left.
   He turn and left.
5. He acted like he didn't see me.
   He acted like he didn't see me.
6. I needed help.
   I need help.
7. He stopped.
   He stop.
8. He called the police.
   He called the police.
9. He stayed with me.
   He stayed with me.
10. He waited for the ambulance.
    He wait for the ambulance.

K. Listen and Write Listen to these sentences from the story. Write the verb you hear. All the verbs are in the regular past tense.

1. Several men jumped out.
2. They mugged me.

3. A short time later, a man passed the alley.
4. I shouted.
5. He turned away.
6. I needed help.
7. He stopped.
8. He called the police.
9. He stayed with me.
10. He waited for the ambulance.

L. Listen and Write Listen to these sentences from the story. Write the verb you hear. All the verbs are in the irregular past tense.
1. They took my coat and my money.
2. They beat me.
3. They left me in an alley.
4. He was from my neighborhood.
5. He never came back.
6. We went to the same church.
7. He wasn't from my country.
8. He saw me in the alley.
9. He felt sorry for me.
10. I thought for a minute.

O. Conversation

Stranger: I just called the police. They'll be here in a minute. What happened?
Man: Some men mugged me.
Stranger: You're hurt. You have a bad cut on your head. But you'll be all right.
Man: My arm. I think it's broken.
Stranger: Just relax. An ambulance is coming.
Man: Can you call my wife?
Stranger: Of course. Give me your number. I'll call after the ambulance gets here.
Man: How can I thank you?

20. Paul

Paul is my wife's cousin. I don't know him well. In fact, we've only met twice in the past fifteen years.

I first met Paul at a family wedding. He wore jeans, no jacket. He was a young man, with long hair down to his waist. Behind his beard was a happy smile. He talked on and on about his life. He lived in a small house in the mountains. There was no heat or electricity. He grew his own food. When he needed a little money, he worked at different jobs for a few weeks. Paul spoke happily about living close to nature. I asked Paul two questions. "How old are you?" "Twenty" was the answer. "Do you have any children?" "No," he laughed. "I'm not married yet."

I met Paul fifteen years later, at another family wedding. This time he wore a suit. His hair was short and he had no beard. But he was still smiling. He talked on and on about his life. He lived in a house near the city. He had a small store and his business was growing. He worked about fifty hours a week. Paul now spoke about the importance of the family. I asked Paul the same two questions. "How old are you now?" "Thirty-five" was the answer. "Do you have any children?" "Yes, " he said. "Four." Then he smiled and said, "Times change."

E. Listen and Number Listen to these sentences from the story. Write the number of the picture in the correct space.
1. I met Paul fifteen years later.
2. He had a small store.
3. He lived in a small house in the mountains.
4. "How old are you now?" "Thirty-five" was the answer.
5. This time he wore a suit.
6. He lived in a house near the city.
7. I first met Paul at a family wedding.
8. He grew his own food.
9. He worked at different jobs for a few weeks.
10. "Do you have any children?" "Yes," he said. "Four."

F. True or False Listen to these statements. Write T if the statement is true, F if the statement is false.
1. Paul is my cousin.
2. Fifteen years ago, he had long hair.
3. Paul talked a lot.
4. Paul lived in the mountains with his family.
5. Paul worked on a farm.
6. As he got older, Paul changed.
7. Paul moved near the city.
8. Paul got married.
9. Paul still has long hair.
10. Paul has four children.

J. Listen and Circle You will hear two sentences. Decide if they are the same or different. Circle "same" or "different."
1. I first met Paul at a family wedding.
   I first meet Paul at a family wedding.
2. He wore jeans.
   He wore jeans.
3. He talk on and on.
   He talked on and on.
4. He lived in a small house in the mountains.
   He lived in a small house in the mountains.
5. He grew his own food.
   He grew his own food.
6. He work at different jobs.
   He worked at different jobs.
7. I ask Paul two questions.
   I asked Paul two questions.
8. He spoke about living close to nature.
   He spoke about living close to nature.
9. "No," he laughed.
   "No," he laughed.
10. He have no beard.
    He had no beard.

K. Listen and Write Listen to these sentences from the story. Write the verb you hear.
1. I first met Paul at a family wedding.
2. He was a young man.

3. He wore jeans.
4. I asked Paul two questions.
5. He had no beard.
6. He talked on and on about his life.
7. He lived in a house near the city.
8. He had a small store.
9. He worked about fifty hours a week.
10. Paul spoke about the importance of the family.

M. Singular or Plural   Listen to these sentences. Is the noun singular or plural? Circle the correct noun.

1. We've only met twice in the past fifteen years.
2. He wore jeans.
3. He lived in a small house in the mountains.
4. There was no heat or electricity.
5. He grew his own food.
6. When he needed a little money, he worked at different jobs.
7. This time he wore a suit.
8. His hair was short.
9. He had a small store.
10. He worked about fifty hours a week.

N. Conversation

Paul: Hi. I'm Paul. I'm Judith's cousin.
Speaker: Oh. Nice to meet you. You live in the country, don't you?
Paul: Yes. I live in the mountains of Colorado.
Speaker: What do you do?
Paul: Oh, I fish, hike, swim, play my guitar, work in my garden.
Speaker: I mean, what do you do for a living?
Paul: Small jobs, like I build tables or paint houses, you know.
Speaker: Sounds like a nice life.
Paul: It sure is. I'd never live in the city.